W9-CDQ-169

Guinea Pigs

JULIE MANCINI

ANIMAL PLANET ♥ PET CARE LIBRARY

Guinea Pigs

Project Team
Editor: Mary E. Grangeia
Technical Editor: Tom Mazorlig
Interior Design: Leah Lococo Ltd. and Stephanie Krautheim
Design Layout: Lundquist Design, New York

TFH Publications®
President/CEO: Glen S. Axelrod
Executive Vice President: Mark E. Johnson
Publisher: Christopher T. Reggio
Production Manager: Kathy Bontz

Discovery Communications, Inc. Book Development Team
Marjorie Kaplan, President and General Manager, Animal Planet Media
Patrick Gates, President, Discovery Commerce
Elizabeth Bakacs, Vice President, Creative and Merchandising
Sue Perez-Jackson, Director, Licensing
Bridget Stoyko, Designer

TFH Publications, Inc.®
One TFH Plaza
Third and Union Avenues
Neptune City, NJ 07753

Printed and bound in China
11 12 13 14 15   11 13 15 14 12 10

Library of Congress Cataloging-in-Publication Data
Mancini, Julie R. (Julie Rach)
  Guinea pigs / Julie Mancini.
     p. cm. – (Animal Planet pet care library)
  Includes index.
  ISBN 0-7938-3769-3 (alk. paper)
  1. Guinea pigs as pets. I. Animal Planet (Television network) II. Title. III. Series.
  SF459.G9M26 2006
  636.935'92–dc22

The Leader In Responsible Animal Care For Over 50 Years!®
www.tfh.com

CENTRAL
Garden & Pet

Table of Contents

Chapter 1

Why I Adore My

Guinea
Pig

Welcome to the exciting and fun-filled world of guinea pig ownership! Guinea pigs are gentle, cuddly pets that enjoy human companionship. They benefit greatly from daily interactions with their owners. With a little training, you may even teach your guinea pig to do simple tricks.

Guinea Pig Origins

Guinea pigs are tailless, plant-eating mammals of the family *Caviidae* that originated in South America. They are relatives of the porcupine and chinchilla and have long been considered rodents.

In 1991, the genetic classification of the guinea pig came into question after an article in *Nature* magazine seemed to suggest they aren't rodents after all. Although most experts still place them in the rodent category, the scientific debate continues.

Guinea Pigs Are Different

Guinea pigs have several key physical differences from other rodents, such as rats and mice. For example, they carry their young for about 68 days, which is about three times as long as some other rodents; their young are born precocious, which means they look like small copies of their parents; and they are ready to care for themselves shortly after birth. Another important difference is that guinea pigs also require additional vitamin C in their diets, which other rodents do not.

Guinea pigs were first domesticated by the Moche people of Peru, who kept them as a food source. They were also used for medicinal purposes and as sacrificial animals. The Moche began domesticating guinea pigs between 2500 and 5000 BC; an exact date is difficult to pinpoint due to a lack of written records or any solid fossil evidence. However, mummified guinea pigs, as well as statues depicting them, have been found in this region of coastal Peru, indicating their strong presence in Moche culture.

Later, early Dutch and British explorers brought them from South America to Europe, where they were raised as exotic pets. Queen Elizabeth I of England was among the first guinea pig owners in Europe.

Relatives of the guinea pig can still be found in the wild. Their habitat range includes forest edges, savannahs, and swamps from Colombia to Argentina. Small groups of these wild guinea pigs live in burrows, foraging for plant materials at night.

A guinea pig is sometimes referred to as a cavy, which is a shortening of his Latin name, *Cavia porcellus*. *Cavia* refers to the guinea pig's scientific family, *Caviidae*, and *porcellus* means little pig. How the guinea pig got his common name is somewhat of a mystery. The pig part of the name seems to come from the squealing noise the animals make from time to time, but the guinea part is a bit more

What's In a Name?

Despite what their common name suggests, guinea pigs are not native to Guinea. Rather, they are found in several regions of South America. They are also referred to as cavies, which is a shortening of their Latin name, *Cavia porcellus*. *Cavia* refers to the guinea pig's scientific family, *Caviidae*, and *porcellus* means little pig.

difficult to pin down. At one time, these animals may have been sold for a guinea in Great Britain. Another possibility is that the name may come from Guyana, a South American country that was once a Dutch colony and a likely export point for the animals to Europe in colonial times. Guyana can easily be mispronounced as Guinea.

Guinea Pig Breeds

The American Rabbit Breeders Association and the American Cavy Breeders Association recognize 13 guinea pig breeds in their Standards of Perfection for show animals. These include Abyssinian, Abyssinian Satin, American, Coronet, Peruvian, Silkie, Teddy, Texel, and White Crested. The American, Peruvian, Silkie, and Teddy are also available in Satin breeds. Satin refers to the sheen or shininess of the animal's coat. Satin animals should have brilliant coats in order to succeed in the show ring.

Both associations have some basic standards that are the same across the board for almost all breeds of guinea pig—the Texel is the exception. All other guinea pigs have a similar body type. The body should be of medium length, with wide, tall shoulders. The

There are many different breeds of guinea pig, each with its own distinct look. Pictured here are a Dalmatian, a Golden Boar, and a Lilac.

shoulders form the tallest part of the guinea pig when you look at his profile. (Texels, on the other hand, have short, cobby bodies.)

The guinea pig's head should be full to the end of his muzzle. The animal should have a Roman nose; well-shaped, somewhat droopy ears; and large, round eyes.

Now that we've discussed the similarities and differences between the breeds, let's look at each breed in a little more detail.

Abyssinian: The Abyssinian's harsh coat is defined by a crisp, symmetrical pattern of rosettes and ridges, and he must have at least eight rosettes in his coat to be shown. The Abyssinian must be able to move about during judging, so his rosettes and ridges can be fully appreciated.

American: The American is a smooth-coated, short-haired, sleek animal. He is the most popular of all the guinea pig breeds and the animal that comes to mind when they are mentioned. The

American was originally known as the English cavy at the time of his recognition by the American Rabbit Breeders Association.

Coronet: The Coronet is known for his long, dense coat, which must be equally long on both sides of his body. The trademark coronet (or crest) must be evenly centered on the animal's forehead. It should have a pinpoint center, and hair should radiate evenly from the coronet.

Peruvian: The Peruvian is known for his dense, soft "sweeps," which can grow several inches long and make it difficult to tell the front end of the animal from the back end. The topknot is called a frontal, and it grows forward, covering the animal's head. When properly groomed, the Peruvian has an oval look when viewed from above. Show animals cannot have their hair trimmed.

Silkie: The Silkie, sometimes called the Sheltie, has a soft, thick coat that grows backward from the

Cavy Characteristics

There are 13 recognized guinea pig breeds. Despite the vast differences in their appearance, certain traits are desirable for all cavies:

- In shape, the body should resemble a brick with rounded corners, with the width of the shoulders in proportion to the hips, and it should be well-fleshed, but not fat.
- The profile of the face should be gently rounded, not straight or ratty, with a full muzzle, flat nose, large, bold eyes, and large petal-shaped ears that droop, set on a broad head.

animal's head. In contrast to the Peruvian, the Silkie's soft coat does *not* naturally part along the back, and it grows backward from the head.

Teddy: The Teddy has a dense, even coat. His hair is unique because the individual hair shafts are bent or kinked, resulting in an erect coat all over the animal's body. The Teddy's coat must also be resilient, which means it should revert to its normal erect look immediately after it is rubbed or otherwise disturbed.

Texel: Originally imported from England, the Texel is easily recognized by his abundant curls. The ideal Texel coat has curls all over the body, even on the belly. These curls should be long and tight. Remember, the Texel is the one breed that is the exception to the normal guinea pig body type—it has a short, cobby, compact build, rather than a medium-length, tall frame.

White Crested: The White Crested is a short-haired, smooth-coated animal with a unique white crest on the top of his head. Show animals can have no other white spots on their bodies—the crest is the only allowable white part of this breed.

Guinea pigs have three basic coat types: long, short, and rough. This Silkie represents a long-haired breed.

Other Breeds: There are some other less recognized breeds. These include the Merino (a long-haired guinea pig with curly hair and a crest on his head), the English self crested (a short-haired guinea pig with a crest that is the same color as the rest of the animal's coat, unlike the White Crested), and the Alpaca (a guinea pig with long, curly hair that grows forward over the head). Other developing breeds include the Lunkara (a long-haired animal with wavy hair), the Silver Marten (a black-and-white version of the tan variety), and the Swiss Teddy (a guinea pig whose appearance resembles that of a powder puff, with uniform-length kinked hair all over his body).

There are also two kinds of hairless guinea pigs. The Baldwin is a totally hairless, wrinkled animal that can be born with some hair, although the hair is lost as the guinea pig matures. The "Skinny Pig" is hairless as well, but often not completely, as there may be patches of hair on the face and paws, as well as fine hair over other parts of the body.

The World's Biggest Guinea Pig

In 2000, scientists working in Venezuela discovered the fossil remains of *Phoberomys pattersoni,* the world's biggest rodent and a distant relative of today's guinea pigs.

"Imagine a weird guinea pig, but huge, with a long tail for balancing on its hind legs, and continuously growing teeth," Marcelo R. Sánchez-Villagra of Germany's University of Tübingen told *Science* magazine. "It was semi-aquatic, like the capybara, and probably foraged along a riverbank."

Phoberomys roamed northern South America about 8 million years ago. He measured about 9 feet (2.7 m) in length, stood more than 4 feet (1.2 m) tall, and tipped the scales at an estimated 1,500 pounds (680.4 kg)—about 700 times the size of most pet guinea pigs today. Scientists theorize he became extinct because his large size made it difficult to avoid predators; he could not burrow his way to safety as many of today's rodents can, and he was unsuited for quick getaways on foot.

Guinea Pigs, Head to Toe

Physical Characteristics

Guinea pigs are stocky little animals that weigh between 1 and 3 pounds (0.5-1.13 kg) at maturity. They have rounded, mostly hairless ears on the tops of their heads; large, round eyes set slightly to the sides of their heads; and flat noses. Their 20 teeth are open-rooted, which means they grow continuously. Guinea pigs have four toes on their front feet and three toes on their back feet.

Depending on the breed of guinea pig you select, your pet may have smooth, short hair, or he may have a kinked, cow-licked, or curly coat. His hair may also flow freely in long locks. It's entirely up to you to determine which coat type you prefer, and your choice should depend on the amount of time your schedule will allow for grooming your pet.

Your guinea pig's coat will fall into one of 23 varieties of color and pattern. These include the single-colored selfs (beige, black, chocolate, cream, lilac, red-eyed orange, red, and white), the banded agoutis (silver, golden, and dilute), the solids (brindle, roan, silver, golden, and dilute), the markeds (broken, Dalmatian, Dutch, Himalayan, tortoiseshell, and tortoiseshell and white) and the tan pattern, which is accepted only in the American breed. Certain varieties— white, roan, broken, Dalmatian, Dutch,

The guinea pig's large, round eyes, flat nose, and pert little ears are just a few of the features that make him a popular pint-sized pet.

Himalayan, and tortoiseshell and white—are not accepted in the White Crested breed.

Coat care for short-haired guinea pigs is relatively simple; occasional brushings will help keep your pet's coat healthy. Long-haired guinea pigs require daily combings to maintain their coats, and they also need special grooming prior to being taken to a show so that their coats will be in top condition. Ask a breeder of long-haired guinea pigs for more information on what type of coat care is required.

The Expert Knows

One Guinea Pig or Two?

Unlike many other small animals that are kept as pets, guinea pigs are sociable animals, which means they are accustomed to being in groups. Simply put: Guinea pigs make better pets if they have piggie pals around. Since you will likely be away from home for long periods during the day (at school or at work), it may be best to have more than one pet guinea pig so the animals can keep each other company. Keep males with males or females with females (or have your animals neutered), unless you want a lot of little guinea pigs running around your home!

How Guinea Pigs Behave

Unlike hamsters and other pocket pets, guinea pigs are diurnal, which means they are awake at the same time as their owners, and they sleep when their owners sleep, although they are known to nap a little in the afternoon.

One of the best qualities about guinea pig behavior is the fact that these little animals are very unlikely to bite. They may nip you gently if you are holding them when they need to eliminate, but they rarely bite hard. Their good temperament makes them easy to care for and handle.

Social little animals, guinea pigs need others of their kind around to be content, so be prepared to keep more than one as a pet. Pair males with males and females with females to keep your piggie population to a manageable number. Guinea pigs breed readily and often, and many new owners don't realize their pets are going to have a litter until the female begins to look very pregnant.

Although guinea pigs aren't as active as mice or hamsters, they do have certain characteristic moves and noises that indicate their moods. These include motor-boating, popcorning, rumblestrutting, and freezing. Freezing seems pretty straightforward, but the other terms may need a little explanation.

Motor-boating describes the cheerful vocalizations a content guinea pig makes as he moves about his cage or explores his surroundings during out-of-cage time. The noises sound similar to those made by a trolling boat motor at low idle.

Popcorning is the animated little dance guinea pigs do when all is right in their world. It can include shivers, shakes, leaps, skips, and jumps, along with chutting vocalizations.

Rumblestrutting is a behavior

Their good temperament makes guinea pigs easy to care for and handle.

It's important to know what behaviors are normal for your guinea pig so you can ensure he is healthy and happy.

that can be used to intimidate other guinea pigs or to attract a mate. The animal will sway at another animal and make a noise that's somewhere between a rumble and a purr.

Other characteristics worth noting include a variety of behaviors used by one guinea pig to show his dominance over others. These can include stiff-legged swaggering, rearing into a fighting stance, fur fluffing to appear larger and more menacing, teeth chattering or clacking, expansive yawning to show off the size of the teeth, and nose or chin raising. Keep a close eye on your guinea pigs—if one

of them starts showing any of these behaviors, a fight may soon break out between two of your pets, and they may need to be separated in order to prevent injury.

Sometimes, it seems as if your guinea pig isn't doing anything at all. This inactivity can also indicate contentment. If he feels comfortable in his surroundings, he's likely to be at ease enough to lounge in his cage or in a favorite spot in your home, such as on the couch or on a pillow on the floor.

Take time to learn those behaviors that are common for your pet. This is an important part of responsible ownership because you'll know quickly when he isn't acting normally, which can be an indication of illness. You'll also know when he's content, when he's frightened, and when he's tired, so you will be able to react to those behaviors promptly to ensure he feels comfortable and secure in your home.

Speaking Their Language

Most guinea pigs are initially shy around people they don't know. Once they become accustomed to their owners, though, they often whistle to

Compared to some pets, a guinea pig's needs are modest—providing good nutrition, a clean home, and daily exercise are well worth the affection you receive in return.

Vocalizations

Guinea pigs use a wide variety of vocalizations to communicate with each other and you. It's important to know what these squeals and chatters mean so you are able to tell if your pet is content or if something is upsetting him.

show their delight at seeing them, and they may purr happily as they are being petted or groomed. Some guinea pigs squeal for attention, while others make the noise only when they are being mishandled or mistreated.

In addition to squealing, guinea pigs have other vocalizations that they use regularly to communicate with each other. As a caring owner, you'll want to know what these noises mean, so you'll be able to tell whether your pet is content in his environment or if something is distressing him. These sounds include chirrups, chuts, chutters, drrrs, purrs, screams, tweets, low wheeks, wheeks, and whines. Let's look at each noise and what it means in a little more detail.

Chirrup: The chirrup can mean several different things to a guinea pig. It may indicate some disturbance or mild upset in his world, or it may be used to attract attention to him.

Chut: The chut is one of the most common guinea pig vocalizations. It indicates that he is content with his home and interested in his surroundings. Guinea pigs chut to one another, and they also chut while exploring their cages or their surroundings during out-of-cage time.

Chutter: Chutters indicate a mildly unhappy guinea pig. He chutters when he does not wish to be bothered by another guinea pig, or when something else is slightly upsetting to him.

Drrr: Guinea pigs drrr when they are startled by a loud noise or something else out of the ordinary in their world. Drrrs are usually followed by the animal freezing in place out of fear.

Purr: Purrs are the opposite of drrrs. Purrs indicate a happy, contented guinea pig that is being petted, or they may indicate a guinea pig in search of a mate. Courting guinea pigs purr to one another as they circle and sway to indicate their interest in each other.

Scream: A scream often indicates that a guinea pig has come out on the losing end of a fight. Screams can also indicate something has frightened a younger animal.

Squeal: As previously indicated, a squealing guinea pig needs attention. He may be in pain, or another guinea pig may be forcing him out of a favored sitting spot or away from a treat bowl.

Tweet: Tweets are usually reserved for young guinea pigs that tweet at their mothers after they have relieved themselves following nursing.

Low Wheek: A low wheeking sound usually means that an owner is on his or her way to clean the cage. Guinea pigs that are separated from their cagemates may also make low wheeking sounds until they are reunited with their buddies.

Wheek: Guinea pigs wheek excitedly when they sense their owners are bringing them food or when they are being let out for some cuddle or play time. They also wheek to communicate with each other as a way of indicating where they are in the home.

Whine: Upset guinea pigs often follow their chuttering with a whine to indicate that they are very unhappy with something in their surroundings.

FAMILY-FRIENDLY TIP

Small Pets for Small Frys

Ideally, a guinea pig can be a child's pet if the parents are willing to carefully supervise the animal's daily care. With adult supervision, children 7 years of age and older can become successful guinea pig owners. If a child does not measure up to this level of responsibility and long-term commitment, a parent should be willing to step in and take over, or it should be considered a family pet, rather than the child's pet.

Hands-On Pets

Regular handling will result in a more cuddly and easily managed pet. Properly handled guinea pigs will become quite affectionate and content to snuggle in the crook of your arm or nuzzle your neck while sitting on your shoulder. They usually develop close bonds with their owners and can live as long as 8-10 years if properly cared for. Remember that they are relying on you to provide them with good nutrition, a clean and comfortable home, daily exercise, and lots of love and attention. Although this may seem like a lot of work at first, once it becomes a part of your daily routine, you'll find that it's easy and well worth the love you get in return. They make wonderful companions for young and old alike!

Male or Female?

In the guinea pig world, opinions are split as to which gender makes the better pet. Some breeders think that male guinea pigs may be friendlier and more sociable than females. Some consider males to be more curious and outgoing, while others don't see a big difference in personality between the genders.

Male guinea pigs can be prone to certain health problems. One of the most common is impaction, in which an older intact male is unable to expel fecal pellets correctly. Males that are not neutered may be prone to fighting and biting one another and may also spray strong-smelling urine in their cages. Neutering tends to solve all of these problems.

Female guinea pigs also have their own set of health concerns. Intact females may be prone to painful ovarian cysts or uterine infections as they age. Both of these conditions can be prevented by spaying the female. Spaying also helps reduce the moodiness some female guinea pigs are prone to as a result of constantly surging hormones.

Growth and Development

When guinea pigs are born, the babies look like smaller versions of the adults.

Guinea pigs make wonderful companions.

When guinea pigs are born, they look like smaller versions of the adults. These babies are a day old.

Their eyes are open, their teeth are in place, and they are fully furred. They can eat solid foods within a few days of birth, although they generally nurse for about three weeks.

Young guinea pigs should remain with their mothers until they are about five weeks old. During this time, mothers teach their offspring about the world, showing them where the food and water bowls are. The youngsters also learn about their surroundings through exploration and play.

As the young guinea pigs mature, they grow independent and move away from their mothers. They start to establish themselves in the pecking order of the group. Females become sexually mature when they are about two months old, and males follow along about a month later.

A guinea pig is considered mature when he is between four and six months of age. If you choose to breed your animals, this is the time to start breeding your females. Females that have not been bred by the time they are six months old may have difficulty delivering their litter because their pelvic bones will have fused together.

Guinea pigs aged four years and older are considered to be "senior citizens." At this point in their lives, they start to slow down physically, and they may become prone to more health problems, such as arthritis, obesity, kidney or liver disease, tumors, dental problems, and respiratory infections.

Life Span

Guinea pigs usually live four to six years, but they can live eight to ten years with good care.

Chapter 2

The Stuff of

Everyday
Life

Before you bring your guinea pig home, you'll need to have a few items on hand to make your new pet feel safe and comfortable when he arrives. These will include a cage, food bowls, water bottles with sipper tubes, some toys, bedding for the cage, and grooming supplies. You may also want to pick up a plastic or wooden house that will fit inside the cage as an additional retreat for him, or you may choose to use a small, clean cardboard box. Guinea pigs appreciate having a quiet place to go to "get away from it all" so they can rest or eliminate without being disturbed.

Housing

Let's look at each accessory in more detail. First and most important is the cage. Your guinea pig will need a habitat in which he feels comfortable and secure. He will need room to roam, but he won't need extra levels or climbing ramps like a hamster or a mouse might. Guinea pigs are fairly horizontal creatures that are not prone to jumping or climbing very high, so it's best to provide them with a large, single-level enclosure.

Sizing Up the Cage

The cage will need to be big enough to accommodate your guinea pig, his food bowl and water bottle, some toys, and a box or hiding house to which he can retreat for naps. Don't shortchange the space in your enclosure because your pet will be spending a fair amount of time in it. Even with ample out-of-cage time, he'll still be inside of it while you're away from home at school or work during the day, so he'll need some room to move around in and explore without feeling cramped.

An ideal cage size for a single guinea pig is 2 feet x 3 feet (0.6 m x 0.9 m), but bigger is always better. The cage should be made out of wire, with a solid bottom that keeps stray litter and other debris contained within the enclosure, but still allows your pet to see what's going on in the room around him. It must have a solid floor to keep your guinea pig from injuring

Guinea Pigs

Selecting Proper Housing

Choosing a proper enclosure is important to the well-being of your pet. Remember that aquariums are designed for fish not mammals. They are a bad choice for guinea pig housing because they are poorly ventilated, which allows excess moisture to build up in the corners of the tank. Also, the smooth glass walls make it awkward to attach necessities such as food bowls, water bottles, and hay racks. Wire cages, available at most pet stores, are recommended.

his feet or legs. Cages with mesh floors or wire bottoms are not recommended.

If you have other pets, you'll need to purchase a solid cage with a secure top that will keep them from having access to your guinea pigs. If they are your only pets, you can purchase a pen or another type of enclosure for them because they are unlikely to climb or jump out.

Place the cage in a room that you use often, like the family room. Your guinea pig is a family pet, after all, and needs to be in a place where he can be part of daily activities. Keeping his cage in the family room, as opposed to a child's bedroom, is ideal for this reason. Also, because it is in a central location, you can check on your pet daily and easily replace food and water as needed. Your guinea pig can come out of his cage to sit with you on the couch as you watch TV, or you can allow him supervised out-of-cage play time in the evenings—which may prove more entertaining than TV!

Keep the enclosure out of direct sunlight to prevent your pet from overheating, and don't hide it in a closet or other completely enclosed area where air cannot circulate around it. Although it may seem like a good idea, keeping your guinea pig in an aquarium or a plastic tub is not ideal. As with the closet, the solid walls of these enclosures do not allow for enough air circulation and are likely to cause your pet to become overheated and possibly ill.

A C&C Cage

An alternative to buying a cage is building a C&C cage, which is made from plastic storage cubes and a corrugated plastic sign board called coroplast. The plastic storage cubes, which can be purchased at many home specialty stores, can be assembled side-by-side to form walls that are held together with snap-fit connectors. The coroplast is sized and cut to create a base on which the walls sit. The walls are easily removed as a unit when the cage needs cleaning, and the coroplast tray is quickly emptied, washed, and refilled with fresh bedding. This type of enclosure offers owners the chance to customize the enclosure size to the number of animals they keep, as well as to their home décor and room specifics. They can become quite elaborate structures.

An ideal cage is well-ventilated and large enough for your guinea pig, his food bowl, water bottle, toys, a hide box, and room for roaming.

The Expert Knows

Attention!

Being a naturally curious and social animal, the more contact a guinea pig has with his family and the daily routine, the happier and more secure he will feel. Therefore, the best location for your pet's cage is in the room your family spends the most time. This way, you can interact with him frequently throughout the day. The more time you spend with your pet after the initial adjustment period, the sooner he will develop a bond of trust with you.

If you choose to construct your own cage with these plastic storage cubes, make sure you purchase ones that measure 14 inches (35.6 cm) square and that have grids that measure less than 1.5 inches (3.81). Larger grids can cause your guinea pig to have sore feet, so it is important to purchase the proper size cubes.

Several guinea pig care websites offer instructions on how to construct these enclosures, and you can find information online by pointing your browser to the search terms "coroplast cube guinea pig."

Cage Furnishings

After you've selected and set up your cage, the first things you'll need to put in it are food bowls and water bottles. Your guinea pig will need two sets of each (more if you're housing several animals per cage). Clean water and fresh food should be available at all times, so it's easiest if you have more than one set of containers on hand. This way, you can remove the used ones at each feeding without having to waste time emptying and washing your feeding accessories at every mealtime. Remember, proper husbandry is essential to your guinea pig's good health.

Clean water bottles and food bowls should be provided at each feeding to ensure your pet's good health.

When selecting a food bowl, make sure it is heavy enough to withstand a hungry guinea pig's weight. Guinea pigs are notorious for standing on or in their bowls while they eat, and plastic bowls are less likely to withstand this kind of treatment. Stoneware bowls are fairly tip-proof, which may make them a good choice. Lightweight plastic bowls can be prone to tipping, so you'll have more replenishing and cleaning up to do if you use them. One clever solution to the tipping problem is to purchase bowls that fit in the corner of the cage and attach to the bars. However, your guinea pig is still likely to climb on his food as he eats, so you may have to change the food more frequently if he eliminates in his bowl.

As far as water bottles go, it's best to give a single guinea pig at least two and to provide one more for each additional guinea pig living in the enclosure (also add one food bowl per guinea pig to keep peace in the cage at mealtime). The reason for doing this is that your pet will still have water if one of the bottles suddenly starts to leak or if it's too difficult for him to get water out of a sipper tube that has tremendous suction. Also check the rubber stoppers on your water bottles regularly, especially if your guinea pig has access to them. Guinea pigs love to chew, and they may nibble on the stoppers and make them less effective at holding water. If this becomes a problem, consider hanging the bottle

Homemade Toy Alternatives

Guinea pigs are easy to entertain, so they are well-suited to playing with homemade toys. Among the items in your home that would provide some fun are paper bags with holes cut in them, clean cardboard boxes, empty oatmeal containers, sheets or balls of newspaper, open lengths of PVC pipe (please make sure the pipe is sized for your pet to crawl through safely or he may get stuck, which will be no fun for either of you), clean socks stuffed with hay, and empty paper towel tubes stuffed with hay or other healthy treats. Some guinea pigs enjoy carrying or throwing plastic kitchenware, so they may like a plastic spoon, empty margarine container, or measuring cup. They are not able to play with their front feet as other rodents do, but they seem to have fun tossing and chasing things around the house.

on the outside of the cage so that only the end of the sipper tube is available to your pet inside the enclosure.

Water bowls are not recommended for guinea pigs because these animals often kick cage litter into their bowls, which would contaminate the water quickly. Bottles are less likely to be fouled than bowls, and they aren't as likely to be knocked over and spilled.

Toys will keep your guinea pig entertained, as well as giving him healthy exercise options.

Clean the water bottles frequently to ensure your pet's good health. Guinea pigs are known to backwash when they drink, which means their water supply can become contaminated if it isn't replaced daily.

Toys and Treats

While toys and guinea pigs might not seem to naturally go together, your pet will need something to play with to help keep him entertained as well as giving him healthy exercise options.

Wooden chew toys are one of the most important cage accessories your guinea pig should have. Access to a number of safe chew toys will ensure his teeth are maintained in top condition. Rotate them regularly, and

make sure to promptly replace any that are worn or chewed through. A guinea pig's teeth grow constantly, and chewing on toys is one of the best ways to help keep them at the proper length. Other chewing options include gourds, cholla wood, or mineral blocks. Try some of these out on your guinea pig to see if he enjoys them. If you notice that his teeth are overgrown, even after he plays with his toys, contact your veterinarian. He or she may need to trim them occasionally to help them stay healthy.

Some guinea pigs enjoy chasing toys, so you may want to see if he likes small plastic balls with bells in them, like the ones usually marketed for cats. He may nose one of these around his cage for hours, or he may enjoy rolling it toward you in a game of "catch" during his out-of-cage time. As mentioned earlier, it is very important to inspect all toys regularly and replace them when they begin to show signs of wear. Guinea pigs can chew through plastic quickly, and you may find yourself with the ball going one way and the bell going another. A better bet may be wire balls with bells inside of them, but these will also have to be checked regularly and replaced when the wire begins to fray. As always, your guinea pig should be supervised while playing with this type of toy.

Guinea pigs often like to see their reflections in a mirror, so you may find that your pet enjoys a mirrored bird toy in his cage. Some have bells on them, which your guinea pig may enjoy ringing as part of his playtime. An added benefit of many bird toys is that they have chewable parts that your guinea pig can use to help maintain his teeth.

Treats may or may not provide some play value. You'll find as you walk down the guinea pig aisle in your local pet supply store that the line between toy and treat can get a little blurry. There are sticks, blocks, bars, salad bowls, and all sorts of chewable goodies that could be toys as well as treats, depending on your point of view. You can also head over to the bird aisle and purchase a treat hanger that allows you to thread various raw vegetables on a metal skewer. Your pets will have a custom-made healthy treat and toy combination when you offer them a kabob of their favorite fresh foods.

No Wheels Necessary

Two things your guinea pig *won't* need are an exercise wheel or an exercise ball. Although both of these toys are popular for hamsters or mice, the anatomy of your guinea pig makes it very difficult for him to use either item safely. If you purchase one for your pet, he will just sit in it and will likely look uncomfortable. A guinea pig's spine is not flexible enough to curve into a comfortable position to run in a ball or on a wheel. In addition to possible spinal damage, he can injure his feet, ankles, or legs, so it's best to leave these toys to pets that can use them and enjoy them.

A House to Hide In

While your guinea pig's cage is technically his house, he'll need an additional retreat inside his enclosure that satisfies his need for privacy and quiet comfort. This retreat offers him a hiding place where he can rest and also go to the bathroom. If he sees or hears something unexpected in your home, chances are he'll escape to his hideout until what he has perceived as danger passes.

For this purpose, you can provide him with a specially made plastic or wooden house or a plastic "pigloo" (an igloo-shaped hiding spot). If you prefer a simpler approach, you can give him a clean, small, cardboard box that doesn't have any large staples in it. Clean the plastic enclosures as needed, and replace the wooden or cardboard ones when they become too dirty or too chewed. If you'll be providing a cardboard hideout for your pet, be sure to cut the bottom out of it so that it won't become soiled when your pet eliminates in it.

Making a Comfortable Home

Before you put your guinea pig in his home, you'll need to provide it with some bedding. Think of bedding as a kind of guinea pig

carpet—it will make the cage warmer for your pet and it will soften the feel of the floor under his feet. Cage bedding also provides an absorbent place for your pet to relieve himself, which he will do in only a few selected spots in the cage, usually in his hiding house. This guinea pig habit helps make your cleanup routine easier.

Your pet will need at least 2 inches (5.1 cm) of bedding on the floor of his cage. He may want more to burrow in, or you may need to add more if you are housing more than one guinea pig per cage.

A wide variety of bedding products await you at the pet supply store.

A hide box offers your guinea pig a place he can retreat to for quiet comfort and security.

Safe Bedding

Shavings are the most popular and economical bedding choice for guinea pigs. Never obtain them from lumberyards or sawmills as they may contain mites and other parasites. Purchase commercially bagged products, like aspen shavings, from your pet shop. Other safe choices can include timothy hay, recycled paper products, hemp fibers, wheat litter, or cellulose.

Bedding choices can include timothy hay, recycled paper products, aspen shavings, hemp fibers, wheat litter, or cellulose. You can also use bath towels as bedding, but these require daily changing and frequent laundering, so you may want to opt for a more disposable material. Timothy hay also requires daily changing to keep the cage clean and to protect your pet's health.

Many guinea pig owners find aspen shavings easy to use and clean up. They absorb liquids pretty well and don't have much of an odor on their own. Recycled paper products and cellulose-based beddings are also popular with many owners because of their absorbent qualities.

Products to avoid are cedar shavings, cat litter, corncob, and straw. Cedar and other soft woods, such as pine, contain phenols, which are aromatic oils that can be irritating to a guinea pig's respiratory system. Cat litter is also not recommended because it lacks the insulating properties of other acceptable cage bedding. Your guinea pig may also try to eat it, which can cause his digestive system to become blocked. Corncob bedding promotes mold growth rather quickly, and it may also be eaten, which can cause digestive blockages like the cat litter. Cat litter and corncob may also hurt your guinea pig's feet because they are both fairly hard materials. Straw does not absorb liquids well and it tends to mold quickly. The sharp stalks may also injure your pet, especially his eyes.

Watch the dust levels of whatever bedding you choose. Some cage bedding can be quite dusty as it comes out of the bag, and your guinea pig may raise more dust while he's rearranging the bedding to suit him. It can also irritate the respiratory system and create allergy problems. You may have to try a few different brands before you find the right one.

The Cleaning Routine

Guinea pigs are easy to keep as pets in part because their cleanup requirements are very straightforward. You'll need just a few basic supplies to keep your pet's cage and surrounding area neat and clean. These include a broom and dustpan, a trash can, a spray bottle filled with a 50/50 vinegar-and-water solution, paper towels, and fresh bedding.

Cage Cleaning Schedule

Daily: Replace food and water, and wash bowls and bottles.
As needed: Remove and replace bedding around food bowls and in bathroom spots at least once midweek.
Weekly: Completely change the cage bedding and inspect and replace toys.

Although you may find commercial cleaning products that are labeled as safe for use on guinea pig enclosures, ask your veterinarian's advice before trying any of them. Some may have strong fumes that could be harmful to your guinea pig, or they may be poisonous if ingested accidentally. For safety's sake, stick with the vinegar-and-water mixture unless your veterinarian tells you to use other products.

Your guinea pig will benefit from a complete change of bedding once a week, along with a spot

Daily cage cleaning is vital to keeping your guinea pig's environment healthy, comfortable, and odor-free.

cleanup or two as the week progresses. The number of spot cleanings needed will be determined by your own pet's habits and the number of guinea pigs you keep in any particular cage.

To clean the cage completely, you'll need to remove your pet and put him in a safe place until you are finished. Then remove his hiding house, toys, food bowls, and water bottles and clean them thoroughly before placing them back in the enclosure. Check his toys for signs of wear, and replace those that seem to be chewed through.

Empty the cage bedding into a trash bag and dispose of it in your garbage or compost pile, as appropriate. Spray the cage with a dilute vinegar-and-water mixture and wipe it down. Use full-strength vinegar on any difficult stains, and allow it to stand 5-10 minutes before wiping it down. Refill the cage with fresh bedding, and replace your pet and his accessories.

For a mini-cleaning, focus your attention on the areas around your guinea pig's food bowl and spots where he eliminates. Remove the cage bedding in these areas with a small dustpan and

It's best to purchase all of your guinea pig's supplies prior to his arrival to make the transition to his new home less traumatic for him.

add fresh bedding as needed. Some owners find it easier to spot-clean the cage every day or every other day as they change the food bowl. It is not necessary to remove your pet from his cage for these quick cleanups. The schedule you select is completely up to you as long as your pet's home stays clean and your pet remains healthy!

Buying Grooming Supplies

Your guinea pig will need to have his coat brushed and his nails clipped regularly to maintain his appearance. Grooming time can also be quality cuddle time, so it helps to make it an enjoyable experience for both of you. While we'll talk about how to use grooming equipment in Chapter 4, this information is being provided here so you'll know what to put on your shopping list before you head to the

pet supply store to purchase your guinea pig's home setup.

Your grooming supplies will include a soft bristle brush (for short-haired guinea pigs), a metal comb or brush (for long-haired guinea pigs), guinea pig or small animal shampoo, a set of nail clippers, a vial of styptic powder, some cotton swabs, a gentle ear cleanser, a pair of scissors, and a towel. If you are planning to show your long-haired guinea pig, you will need to purchase a set of wraps and learn how to prepare his coat for a show. Ask the breeder or store from whom you purchased your pet for more information on how to wrap his hair properly.

Consider keeping all of your supplies in a plastic box so that they are handy when it's grooming time. If you don't want to keep them in a box, you may want to place them on a shelf near your pet's cage so they are easily accessible.

FAMILY-FRIENDLY TIP

Responsible Pet Ownership

Guinea pigs can be ideal pets for children—if parents are willing to be involved in the daily care and maintenance of the animal and his cage.

- Children who are 7 years of age or older are usually able to handle the responsibility of caring for a guinea pig with parental supervision. However, parents need to make sure the guinea pig has fresh food and water on a regular schedule and that his cage is cleaned routinely. They must also supervise out-of-cage time so that the pet enjoys it as much as his family does.

- Parents should never use a guinea pig—or any pet—to teach a child about responsibility. If a child does not take proper care of the pet, only the pet suffers. It's not fair to the animal to be treated this way, so please don't do it!

- Use extra caution when handling and carrying young guinea pigs. They are quite energetic and are prone to wiggling and trying to escape from the hands that carry them, so it may be best for adults to do most of the handling until the pets are mature.

Your Guinea Pig's First Day in Your Home

New pets are a lot of fun, and there's no denying that. However, you should take some time to think about how your guinea pig is feeling as he becomes part of your family. The first day he comes to your home is probably an exciting one for both of you, but your pet's excitement is likely to shift to stress very quickly. So, it's best to keep his activities to a minimum for the first few days.

Look at the world from your pet's point of view: he's in an unfamiliar place with unfamiliar people making all sorts of noise. Remember that your guinea pig is naturally considered a prey animal, which means that it may be easy for him to interpret things you normally do (like trying to take him out of his cage) as a threat to his health and well-being. Prey animals have to deal with the constant peril of being eaten in the wild and, even though your guinea pig is not a wild animal, his natural instincts are still the same. They are telling him that he's in a potentially dangerous place until he gets used to your home and your routine.

After you put your guinea pig in his new cage, let him stay in it for a day or two to adjust to the sounds and activities in your home. Sit beside the cage and talk to him so he gets to know your voice. Tell him about your family and how happy you are that he's part of it now. Reassure him that he's in a safe place where people will take good care of him, and then let him settle in.

After a day or so, you can take your pet out of his home and allow him to sit on your lap. Don't chase him around the cage with your hand; remember, these gestures seem threatening to a guinea pig, no matter how harmless and practical they are to us. If you seem to be chasing him around the cage and stressing him, stop what you're doing, let him calm down, and try a new approach. First, show him your hands and explain that you don't mean him any harm. Offer him a treat to entice him to come over to you, then gently pick him up with both hands and carry him to a safe spot on the couch or floor.

The Guinea Pig's Activity Cycle

Fortunately for owners, guinea pigs are on a diurnal schedule. This means they are awake when we are awake, and they sleep when we sleep. They eat at about the same times that we do, although guinea pigs will often snack throughout the day instead of eating formal meals.

Try to set up a routine for your pet so he will know when to expect meals and out-of-cage time. This schedule doesn't have to be set in stone, but certain activities like feeding should occur around the same time each day. Setting a schedule ensures that your pet receives the daily care he needs, along with some fun time for both of you.

At first, keep the room environment fairly quiet to let your pet adjust to your home and family. Don't have a stereo blasting in the corner or let the kids start a wrestling match on the

Gentle, consistent handling and attention are the keys to helping your pet adjust to his new home.

floor as you take your guinea pig out for the first time. Gentle, consistent handling and attention are the keys to helping your pet adjust. With patient, kind treatment, he should soon fit into your home and become a welcome member of the family.

On a related note, please don't give a guinea pig as a present for birthdays, Christmas, or Hanukkah. Holidays are exciting enough on their own, and they will only add to a guinea pig's stress level if he is introduced to a new home on such a busy occasion. If you want to give a guinea pig as a gift, assemble a selection of care products and present those instead, along with a gift certificate that can be redeemed later on when your home life is less hectic.

Keeping Your Guinea Pig Safe

Before you let your pet loose for his out-of-cage time, be sure that the room he'll be playing in and exploring has been pet-proofed. This process is similar to baby-proofing a room to protect wandering young children from harm, and it's important to take the time to do this before letting your guinea pig out of his cage.

First, close up any gaps under or behind furniture. Guinea pigs are naturally curious and they love quiet, dark places, so it's best to prevent them from having access to the space behind the couch or under the bed (unless you like moving furniture a lot!). Also, hide electrical cords in PVC piping or tack it out of your guinea pig's reach to prevent him from chewing on them.

Block the playroom's doorway with a piece of board approximately 1 foot (0.3 m) high and a little wider than the door frame. This will help keep your guinea pig safely inside the room. If you have other pets in the home, you may want to add a baby gate to this door blocker to protect him from unexpected

Before your guinea pig has out-of-cage time, be sure the area he'll be playing in and exporing has been pet-proofed. Never leave him unsupervised—indoors or out.

visits from the other animals. Also, it's a good idea to remove pets from the same location when your guinea pig is out and about. Cats and dogs have the ability to harm them unintentionally by biting or clawing them, so it's best to keep them away.

Tell family members or guests when you let the guinea pig out so he isn't accidentally stepped on or sat on by a careless person. Check couch cushions carefully before sitting down so you don't accidentally squash your pet. Some guinea pigs like to make play tunnels under area rugs and hallway runners, so tread carefully.

Finally, and most important, supervise your pet whenever he's out of his cage. He'll be safer, and everyone will be able to enjoy a little quality pet-and-owner time together!

Plants that are toxic to your guinea pig are commonly found in your home and backyard, so make sure he doesn't have access to them.

33

The Great Outdoors

If you're thinking about providing your guinea pig with his own outdoor pen, choose your location carefully. Be sure you set your pet up on grass that has not been treated with chemical fertilizers or insecticides and that it has not recently been visited by other pets or wild animals that may have eliminated on it. Guinea pigs can become seriously ill if they consume contaminated grass, so be very careful.

If the temperature outside is above 80°F (26.7°C), consider keeping your guinea pig inside. They are prone to heat stress and heatstroke—it's one of the most common emergency conditions veterinarians treat in these pets. You'll want to watch the temperature and humidity carefully to protect him from harm. Also, provide him with ample shade and plenty of fresh water to help keep him cool.

Finally, supervise your pet carefully whenever he's outdoors. Predators such as stray cats, birds of prey, coyotes, or raccoons can quickly take a guinea pig, so you must be vigilant about protecting your pet.

Chapter 3

Good Eating

Now that you know the basic accessories your guinea pig requires to live comfortably in your home, it's time to discuss his diet. Proper nutrition is an important aspect of your guinea pig's daily needs, not to mention these animals love to eat!

G uinea pigs are herbivores. In their native South American homelands, they eat a variety of plant materials to obtain the nutrients they need to live healthy lives. Their digestive system metabolizes food quickly, and they eat almost constantly. Guinea pigs forage for grasses, roots, fruits, and seeds in the late afternoon and early evening. They do not require meat or dairy products in order to maintain good health. In fact, it's not a good idea to feed them either of these types of food because they cannot digest them properly.

Basic Dietary Needs

Let's look at the basic nutrients your guinea pig needs to maintain his good health. He needs a diet that contains the proper amounts of protein, fat, fiber, and trace minerals, such as calcium, and he needs supplemental vitamin C. When guinea pigs were first kept as pets, they were likely fed kitchen scraps with some fresh vegetables thrown in. (Guinea pigs that live in rural parts of South America are still fed that way.) Somehow, through sheer luck and some good accidental combinations of leftovers, they grew and reproduced.

Today, guinea pigs are fairly easy to maintain because their dietary needs are easily fulfilled with a quality food pellet, some fresh fruits and vegetables, clean timothy or grass hay, and fresh water. Along with providing optimal nutrition, feeding a pelleted diet makes keeping these animals very easy.

Pellets provide the right balance of trace minerals, protein, fat, and fiber in your guinea pig's diet, all packaged in a neat, easy-to-serve form. Most commercially available types contain between 16 and 20 percent protein and 16 percent fiber. This is a good balance for adults. Growing, pregnant, or recuperating guinea pigs may have different dietary requirements than adult animals. Discuss the special needs of these animals with your veterinarian to ensure you're feeding your pet the right food to help him grow, heal, or maintain his good health.

The Importance of Vitamin C

When selecting a food pellet for your pet, make sure that you purchase one

Additional Vitamin C

Do not try to supplement your pet's vitamin C needs by adding it to his drinking water. Vitamin C degrades quickly in water, which means you'll need to change it more frequently, and it may make it taste funny or unfamiliar, which can make your pet reluctant to drink. If your guinea pig needs supplemental vitamin C in addition to what he receives in his diet, discuss those needs with your veterinarian. A chewable form may be necessary to get his level back where it belongs.

The guinea pig's nutritional needs are easily met with a quality food pellet, some fresh fruits and vegetables, clean hay, and fresh water.

formulated specifically for guinea pigs. These pellets will contain supplemental vitamin C, which your pet needs because his body cannot manufacture it on its own. Like humans, guinea pigs are one of only a few mammals that require supplemental vitamin C in their diets to maintain good health. A healthy adult needs 15 to 25 milligrams of vitamin C each day, while pregnant females need 30 milligrams. Ill or injured guinea pigs may need up to 100 milligrams daily to help them recuperate. Rabbit or hamster pellets do not contain vitamin C, and they may be supplemented with antibiotics that can harm your guinea pig's health. (Many antibiotics are toxic to guinea pigs.) Your guinea pig has a delicate balance of beneficial bacteria in his digestive system to help him process food properly, and feeding him inappropriately will upset this balance and may cause him to become ill.

Purchase small quantities of food to ensure freshness. Select only products that have an expiration date on them so you can judge this effectively. Vitamin C remains in pellets for two to three months after manufacture, so food older than that will not be as healthful for your pet. Store it in a cool, dark place to help maintain its freshness and effectiveness.

Variety

Introduce your guinea pig to several varieties of pellet when he is young so he will be accustomed to eating more than one type of food. It's important to do this so he doesn't become too fond of one single brand. Guinea pigs can become quite set in their ways where food is concerned, and they may refuse to eat if they are suddenly faced with a change. Think what might happen if your chosen food company went out of business or if you moved to another part of the country where your pet's favorite pellet brand might not be available. Take steps to prevent such problems by alternating between two or three types.

Some pellet brands contain only hay-based greenish brown pellets, while others contain several different colors and shapes of pellets, supplemented with dried fruits and vegetables. Learn which type your pet prefers by purchasing small bags of each and trying them out on your pet. Some guinea pigs will be content with simple pellets, supplemented by your own fresh fruit and vegetable choices, while others will have more wide-ranging palates and will relish the fancier foods.

You may want to steer clear of diets that contain seeds or nuts. Guinea pigs are not accustomed to eating either of them, and they may pose a choking hazard. Also, diets with these ingredients may cause them to pack on the pounds because of their higher fat content.

Read the label on your pet's food carefully. It should not include any of the following ingredients: animal products, beet pulp, corn products, rice bran or rice flour, or vegetable fiber. These are fillers that add nothing healthful to your pet's diet. The food pellets you select should

Pellet foods contain necessary vitamins and nutrients in an easy-to-feed form. Be sure to offer only those specifically made for guinea pigs.

Hay, an important dietary supplement, provides long fiber and aids in the proper digestion of food.

also not contain sweeteners such as corn syrup or sucrose, artificial coloring, or preservatives such as ethoxyquin, propylene glycol, propyl gallate, potassium sorbate, sodium nitrate, sodium nitrite, sodium metabisulfate, butylated hydroxyanisole (BHA), or butylated hydroxytoluene (BHT). Again, these are ingredients that are not healthy for your guinea pig.

Be aware of the calcium levels in your guinea pig's diet, too. Excessive levels of calcium can lead to the formation of bladder stones, which can be a serious health problem. A guinea pig with a bladder stone may hunch over in his cage, vocalize when he urinates, pass bloody urine, or may be unable to urinate at all. If you see any

of these signs of trouble, call your veterinarian immediately for an evaluation. Surgery may be required to treat this problem effectively. If left untreated, your pet could die from

Foods to Avoid!

Certain foods are not healthy for your guinea pig or may be toxic to him. These include:

- avocado
- chocolate
- dairy products
- iceberg lettuce
- meat
- onions
- potatoes
- raw beans
- shelled nuts or seeds

complications relating to bladder stones. Guinea pigs that have had bladder stones will benefit from grass hay and grass hay-based pellets in their diets.

Hay! Hay! Hay!

One vital dietary supplement your guinea pig needs is hay. Hay provides long fiber that helps to keep intestines healthy. It also keeps teeth worn down evenly. Remember that your guinea pig's teeth are constantly growing, and it's important for them to wear evenly so he can continue to eat normally. Hay also substitutes for the plants and grasses guinea pigs have fed on in their natural environments down through time.

Different types of hay can be purchased at pet supply stores, feed stores, horse stables, or from online retailers. Some of the varieties you may encounter include Bermuda grass, Kentucky blue grass, brome grass, clover, fescue, oats, rye, and wheat. Hay breaks down into two general classes: grass hay or legume hay. Grass hay is made by drying grasses and can be identified by long thin blades, while legume hay is made from alfalfa or clover and looks a lot like clover leaves.

Two of the most common hay types are timothy and alfalfa. Timothy hay, a

Small Portions

Although guinea pigs always appear ravenous, they do not eat to the point of gluttony; they feast only until they are full. Any uneaten food should be removed from the cage each day. To avoid waste, feed a small handful of fresh vegetables and fruit two or three times daily, preferably at regular intervals, rather than a large amount at once. This will keep food fresh and clean, as well as prevent it from molding. Always wash foods before feeding them to your pet.

grass hay, is recommended for adult guinea pigs because it gives them adequate levels of protein, fiber, and minerals. Alfalfa hay, a legume hay, contains higher levels of calcium and protein than timothy, so it should be fed only to growing or pregnant guinea pigs, rather than to healthy adult animals. (Alfalfa hay may cause bladder stones in adults. If you can't select timothy hay for some reason, choose another grass hay over a legume hay.)

Offer fresh, clean hay to your guinea pig daily, either by providing him with handfuls of it in his cage or by giving him hay cubes on which he can chew. Remove well-chewed or soiled hay from the cage as part of your daily cleanup routine. Guinea pigs also enjoy sleeping and playing in it, so consider using hay as a cage liner.

Purchase the freshest hay possible. It should be dry and have a clean, sweet smell. Fresh hay should not be dusty. Also, check for mold, which can lead to health problems if consumed. Consider purchasing hay by the bale at your local feed store if you have a lot of guinea pigs in your home. If you have only a few, consider using mail order sources because their supply may be fresher that what's available in your local pet supply store.

When storing hay, remember that it has to stay dry in order to prevent it from becoming moldy and unhealthy. Keep it out of the sun and off the ground to allow air to circulate under it and maintain its freshness. Don't store hay in a plastic container because plastic draws moisture, which can encourage mold growth. Specially designed hay bags (also called bale covers) are available from pet supply or feed stores.

Fresh Foods to Feed

Fruits and vegetables, in appropriate amounts, can be wonderful additions to your guinea pig's diet. They can provide him with something different to chew on other than his normal pelleted diet, and they can give him the vitamin C he needs to maintain good health.

When making fresh food choices

Fresh fruits and vegetables are indispensable in keeping your guinea pig's diet balanced and providing him with the vitamin C he needs.

for your pet, keep the vitamin C levels of particular vegetables and fruits in mind. Consult the United States Department of Agriculture's National Nutrient Database (available online at www.nal.usda.gov/fnic/foodcomp) for a list of foods that have a high vitamin C content.

Among the best fresh foods you can feed your guinea pig are cooked dark-green leafy vegetables, such as kale, turnip greens, or collard greens. Other nutritious offerings include orange slices, brussel sprouts, slivers of raw red or green peppers, guavas, broccoli leaves, slices of kiwi fruit,

Like humans, guinea pigs cannot manufacture their own vitamin C. Many health problems that affect them can be traced to deficiencies, so be sure that your pet consumes an adequate amount. The following is a list of the top 30 fruits and vegetables with good vitamin C content. The last number in each listing shows the milligrams contained in the serving size:

fresh sweet red peppers, 1 cup/283.1

fresh sweet green peppers, 1 cup/119.8

fresh strawberries, 1 cup/97.6

fresh oranges, 1 cup/95.8

fresh papaya, 1 cup/86.5

raw broccoli, 1 cup/78.5

fresh kiwi fruit, 1 medium kiwi/70.5

fresh cantaloupe, 1 cup/58.7

fresh pineapple, 1 cup/56.1

fresh mangos, 1 cup/45.7

cooked Chinese cabbage, 1 cup/44.2

raw red cabbage, 1 cup/39.9

cooked turnip greens, 1 cup/39.5

fresh white grapefruit, 1/2 grapefruit/39.3

fresh pink or red grapefruit, 1/2 grapefruit/38.4

cooked beet greens, 1 cup/35.9

cooked mustard greens, 1 cup/35.4

cooked collards, 1 cup/34.6

fresh raspberries, 1 cup/32.2

cooked rutabagas, 1 cup/32.0

fresh honeydew melon, 1 cup/30.6

fresh blackberries, 1 cup/30.2

fresh watermelon, 1 wedge/23.2

fresh tomatoes, 1 cup/22.9

fresh cabbage, 1 cup/22.5

fresh summer squash, 1 cup/19.2

cooked dandelion greens, 1 cup/18.9

cooked turnips, 1 cup/18.1

cooked spinach, 1 cup/17.6

fresh red or green grapes, 1 cup/17.3

Vitamin Supplement Caution

If you feed your pet a well-balanced diet that includes proteins, carbohydrates, and vitamins, you should have no need to supply concentrated supplements. Your guinea pig may benefit from supplemental vitamin C in the form of chewable tablets from time to time. However, be aware that an excess of any vitamin or mineral can be harmful to your pet because it can upset the absorption rate of other compounds. Discuss your pet's diet with your veterinarian to determine whether or not he needs supplementation.

Wash all fresh foods thoroughly before serving them to your pet to ensure they are free of pesticide residue or bacterial contamination. Remove seeds from apples and other fruits so your pet doesn't accidentally eat them; some seeds are harmful to guinea pigs, and all seeds pose a potential choking hazard.

Scurvy

If your guinea pig does not receive adequate vitamin C in his diet, he may be prone to a disease called scurvy, which is a disease of the bones and cartilage. Clinical signs of scurvy include sudden bleeding, swollen joints, loss of appetite, reluctance to

raw parsley sprigs, and cooked mustard or dandelion greens. You can also feed fresh raspberries, tomatoes, and asparagus.

Certain vegetables listed above, such as cabbage, collards, Chinese cabbage, cauliflower, and broccoli should be offered to your guinea pig only as occasional food items due to their tendency to cause flatulence.

For special treats, you can give your guinea pig small pieces of fruit, such as apples or bananas. He may also enjoy slices of papaya, pineapple, or mango. Unsweetened orange juice or cranberry juice may also be offered in small quantities (this is another way to boost the vitamin C level in the diet).

Your guinea pig should have access to fresh, clean water at all times.

Good Eating

The Importance of Water

Water is a vital part of your guinea pig's daily diet. It helps to deliver vital nutrients to the cells in his body, and it removes waste. Water also helps to keep your pet hydrated and healthy. Offer fresh water daily in a clean water bottle with a sipper tube. Do not use distilled water or water that contains high levels of minerals. Any tap water that is safe for you to drink should be fine for your pet. Water dishes are not recommended for guinea pigs because they are too easily contaminated with bedding or other cage debris as your pet scampers around his home.

To help maintain your pet's good health, wash and rinse the bottle daily to ensure it remains free of mold and germs, and inspect it regularly to make sure your pet isn't chewing on the stopper and causing it to leak. Keep in mind that some guinea pigs tend to backwash food into their water bottles, so it's essential to clean your pet's water bottle every day.

move, loose teeth, and painful lumps along the rib cage. If not treated, scurvy can be fatal to a guinea pig.

You should get in the habit of checking for scurvy because it's important to treat this disease right away. Look at the teeth and gums regularly to make sure they look healthy. Feel gently along his rib cage for any lumps or bumps. If your pet suddenly develops these conditions, contact your veterinarian's office for an immediate appointment.

Watch for Oxalic Acid!

Another item to be aware of in your guinea pig's diet is the amount of oxalic acid certain foods contain. Guinea pigs that are exposed to high levels of dietary oxalic acid may develop crystals in their urine that could lead to urinary tract blockage and kidney damage. Oxalic acid also binds with calcium, which can make this necessary mineral unusable.

The USDA has prepared a chart of oxalic acid levels in certain vegetables, which you can find online at http://www.nal.usda.gov/fnic/foodcomp

Creatures of habit, guinea pigs like to be fed at the same time every day, so stick to a set schedule.

/Data/Other/oxalic.html. Foods with high oxalic acid that may be unsuitable for your guinea pig include beet greens, Swiss chard, amaranth, cassava, purslane, and chives. However, other oxalic acid-rich foods, such as spinach, parsley, and kale, are important additions to your guinea pig's diet because they contain high levels of vitamin C and can be fed in moderation.

The key to proper feeding is learning what elements different foods contain and balancing the amount your pet receives in his diet. Discuss your pet's nutritional requirements with your veterinarian to ensure you're feeding him the healthiest diet possible.

Feeding Schedule

Offer your guinea pig fresh foods in the morning so you can remove them from the cage before he goes to bed at night. This will help keep the cage cleaner and will make your pet less likely to become ill from eating moldy or rotten food.

Along with the fresh foods, check your guinea pig's water bottle in the morning to ensure it isn't leaking and that he has plenty of water. Guinea pigs need at least 30 milliliters (0.9 ounces) of water per pound each day to maintain good health. When you offer your pet his evening meal, change the water and wash the bottle out to ensure the water doesn't become

moldy or stale. Clean the water tube, also, to prevent bacteria buildup, especially in the elbow area where it bends to fit into the cage.

Offer 1/8 cup of pellets daily, and remove them after about an hour. If you see that he leaves food in his dish, cut back a little; if he seems hungry all the time, add a little more to his next meal. Over time, you'll learn what the right amount of food is for your pet.

Feeding the Finicky Eater

Many guinea pigs are ready and willing eaters, but others are more particular about their food preferences. If you have a finicky eater at your house, be patient with him. Continue to offer a

FAMILY-FRIENDLY TIP

Kids Can Help at Feeding Time

A child can help feed a guinea pig by offering fresh foods to the animal each day under adult supervision, or he or she can help a parent fill up the pellet dish and change the water bottle at mealtime. Although kids should not be the only ones responsible for feeding the guinea pig, it's a good idea to have them take an active daily role in this part of the animal's care.

Healthy Treats

Your guinea pig will enjoy occasional treats. These can include guinea pig-sized portions of:

- apple slices
- banana slices
- berries, such as strawberries, raspberries, or blackberries
- commercially available guinea pig treats
- grapes
- mango slices
- papaya slices
- pineapple chunks
- rolled oats
- unsweetened dry cereal

Limit the amount of commercial guinea pig treats your pet eats to help him maintain his weight and good health.

wide variety of foods to try to tempt him out of his picky habits, but do so gradually because some animals can stop eating altogether if you start changing their menu too dramatically.

If you have more than one guinea pig, enlist the help of your other pets to show the fussy eater that new and different foods can be tasty. You may not have a problem with a finicky eater because some good-natured eating competition may occur between your guinea pigs as they race to see who can finish their food first! Feed the less picky eaters first, and praise them for being such good eaters. Offer a similar portion of new foods to your picky eater and encourage him to try them, but be sure to give him old favorites as well to maintain his appetite. In time, you may find that your fussy eater has become less picky. If he continues to be

Although many types of treats are available, be sure to offer healthy ones in small amounts.

Guinea pigs have healthy appetites, so a loss of interest in food may signal an illness or dental problems.

set in his ways when it comes to mealtime, accept the fact and appreciate him for his other wonderful qualities.

Maintaining a Healthy Weight

On the other end of the spectrum from the finicky guinea pig is the one that will eat anything. In many cases, such cooperative eaters usually end up as plump and pudgy pets! These animals should be given adequate opportunities to exercise (supervised out-of-cage time is an ideal way for them to run around, burn off some calories,

and explore the room in which they live) and fed additional timothy hay to help fill them up without adding extra calories to their diets. Feed timothy hay-based pellets, also, to provide them with proper nutrition without adding too much protein or fat to their daily regimens.

Weigh your guinea pig weekly to ensure his good health. Purchase a kitchen scale that weighs in grams, and train your pet to sit in it during weigh-ins. Lavish praise on him and add a few special treats, such as an apple slice or a few chunks of carrot, which will make it a fun event as well as encouraging him to sit still. Keep a written record so you will know if he's maintaining a healthy

Determining the proper diet and optimum nutrition depends on your guinea pig's age and gender.

48

Guinea Pigs

weight or if he's getting too fat or too thin.

Healthy adult guinea pigs weigh between 700 and 1200 grams (that's between 24.5 and 42 ounces, or 1.5 and 2.6 pounds). The weight for females ranges between 700 and 900 grams, while males weigh between 900 and 1200 grams. If you aren't sure what your guinea pig's weight should be, call your veterinarian's office to ask if they can check his records and tell you what he weighed at his last routine examination. Discuss his weight to determine if he's underweight, and find out what foods he can eat to help him boost his weight. If he's a bit

overweight, learn what you can do in terms of changing his diet and exercise routine to help him trim down.

When Your Guinea Pig Doesn't Want to Eat

In addition to monitoring your pet's weight each week, keep an eye on his appetite each day. Make sure he's eating about the same amount of food and drinking the same amount of water daily. Take notice if he suddenly loses interest in food or seems to sit sadly by his dish without eating, because these behaviors can indicate a health problem that requires veterinary attention. Healthy guinea pigs have

Coprophagy

Although it may be a little unpleasant to think about or discuss, guinea pig owners need to be aware that their pets will eat their own droppings from time to time. This habit is called coprophagy.

Because guinea pigs are one of the smallest grass-eating mammals, they do not have a long digestive system to assist them in processing their food. To help maintain the bacterial balance in their digestive tract, they occasionally consume special soft waste pellets called cecotropes, which contain B vitamins and bacteria needed to maintain healthy digestion and to process their hay-based diet effectively. Cecotrope pellets are not the same as regular feces and must be consumed to maintain good health. Do not discourage your guinea pig from doing this.

hearty appetites, and loss of interest in food is one of the main signs of illness in your pet.

Health problems that cause appetite loss include scurvy, overgrown or misaligned teeth, respiratory problems, and digestive system upsets. Some of these can become very serious illnesses if left untreated.

Guinea pigs naturally hide signs of illness because they are prey animals, and animals that show any sign of weakness are often eaten. This tendency to hide illness makes it extra important for you as a caring owner to pay attention to your pet's behavior and actions. The longer a guinea pig remains ill, the less likely he will be to make a complete recovery, so take immediate action if your pet stops eating.

Good Eating

Weigh your pets often to see if they are maintaining a healthy weight.

Looking Good

Grooming is an important part of your responsibilities as a guinea pig owner. Regular grooming not only keeps a guinea pig looking good, but it helps to keep him feeling good. The hands-on routine also gives you an opportunity to detect subtle changes in your pet's appearance or body that may signal a health problem.

uinea pigs spend part of their day grooming themselves and each other, but they can use a little help from their owners to ensure their coats are in tip-top shape. Grooming can also be social time for you and your pet, so make the most of it.

Brushing

Brushing should be an important part of your guinea pig's daily routine. It adds sheen and luster to his coat, which makes him look prettier and healthier. Try to brush your pet every day to give him some special attention and to help remove dead hairs and bits of bedding or food from his coat.

To begin grooming your guinea pig, start brushing him at the back of his head and work down his back using a soft-bristled brush (on a short-haired guinea pig). Brush him in the direction his hair grows, down his back and

Regular grooming not only keeps your guinea pig looking good, but it improves his overall hygiene.

under his rump. Be gentle and take the time to work out any tangles without pulling on them too hard. After you brush his back, brush his sides and

Haircuts for Long-Haired Guinea Pigs

Owners of long-haired guinea pigs should plan on giving their pets bimonthly haircuts to keep their coats in top condition. Regular trimming keeps the coat from tangling, and it also helps prevent urine and feces from becoming caught in the hairs around your pet's bottom. This should be done every 8-12 weeks.

To trim your long-haired guinea pig, first gather your grooming tools; you'll need a sharp pair of scissors and a metal comb to work out any mats or tangles. Place your pet on your lap, and play with him to make him feel comfortable. After he's settled in, comb the top half of his hair to remove mats, then hold a small section between the fingers of one hand (as hairdressers do) and trim off the ends with the scissors. You may be able to do only one or two sections at a sitting, or your pet may be calm enough for you to trim about half his hair at one time. Trim it short enough so your pet isn't dragging it through his cage litter. Trim him again when his hair has grown out.

legs using the same gentle stroke.

If your pet has long hair, use a metal comb for grooming. Pin brushes or slicker brushes also work well on long-haired guinea pigs because the stiffness of the bristles allows you to brush through tangles instead of gliding over them as a soft-bristled brush would. Ask for recommendations at your pet supply store as to which type of grooming tool you'll need to keep your long-haired guinea pig's coat in condition.

As you groom your pet, inspect his body and be aware of any dry patches or parasites on his skin. Guinea pigs can be prone to a variety of skin problems, including fleas, mites, lice, or fungus—all of which require veterinary care to be treated effectively. Most of these will not occur if your pet is kept in a clean cage and fed a balanced diet, but it's important to report any changes to your veterinarian promptly in case there is a problem.

Both long- and short-haired guinea pigs should be groomed daily. Regular brushing will help keep tangles to a minimum, and all guinea pigs will benefit from the special attention they receive from their owners during grooming time.

Long-haired guinea pigs or breeds that have more unusual coats will require a little more care during brushing. For example, the hair of an Abyssinian grows in swirls to form rosettes all over the body, so they need to be brushed in the direction these rosettes grow, which can be challenging for some owners because

FAMILY-FRIENDLY TIP

Remember to Brush

Children can help groom a guinea pig by gently brushing him under adult supervision. After demonstrating that they can handle the animal carefully without harming him, they can be allowed to groom him regularly. Children can also look at a guinea pig's eyes or ears to see if they need cleaning and let an adult know if this type of attention is needed. Responsibilities can be added as the child matures.

there are so many of them. Peruvians may need to have their long hair wrapped to train it properly for the show ring. This is usually done by wrapping the hair around small, flat pieces of balsa wood surrounded by tissues and holding them in place with rubber bands prior to the event. If you decide to show your animal, you can call the breeders association or go online to find out more about what's involved.

Bathing

Bathing is not normally part of a guinea pig's grooming routine, but it's important to discuss the topic in case you have to give your pet a bath at some point.

53

Looking Good

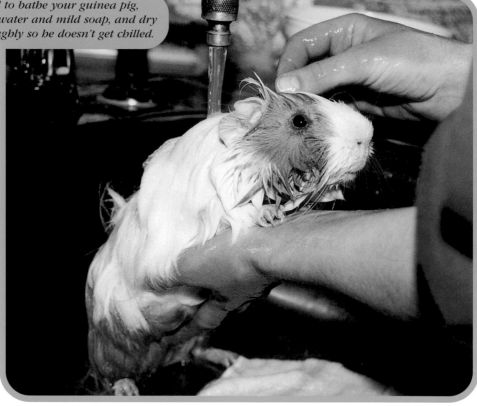

If you need to bathe your guinea pig, use warm water and mild soap, and dry him thoroughly so he doesn't get chilled.

First, use only a guinea pig or small animal shampoo—those formulated for people or for other pets are probably too harsh for your guinea pig's coat. Wash him in a small sink so you can maintain control of him during the bathing process.

Use warm water and a small amount of shampoo. Keep soap out of his eyes and ears. Support his body by placing one hand under his front legs, and use the other to wash and rinse him. Be sure to hold on to your pet during the bath because he will be slippery! Also,

you will probably have better luck bathing him if you keep his front feet from touching the bottom of the sink. If he can get all four feet on the ground, he may be likely to try to run away, which will make the experience more difficult and less pleasant for both of you.

Rinse all of the shampoo from your guinea pig's coat and pat him with a towel to absorb excess water. Then, wrap him in another small, dry towel and remove him from the sink, remembering to support his body with both hands.

If you think you are ready to trim your guinea pig's nails at home, the following instructions will help you do so safely:

1 To trim your pet's nails, you will need a regular set of small pet nail trimmers. Don't use scissors—they will crush your pet's nails. You will also need some styptic powder in case a nail is cut too deeply.

2 If your pet is used to having his nails trimmed, settle him onto your lap and hold one of his feet in your hand. If he is not accustomed to this treatment, it may work better to have an assistant hold your pet while you do the trimming—guinea pigs can sometimes wiggle at the wrong time, which may cause you to cut deeper than you intended. You may also want to wrap your guinea pig in a small towel and have only his feet sticking out to make nail trimming easier.

3 Look for a pink or red line in the middle of your pet's nail. This is the quick, or the blood supply, and you don't want to cut this because it will hurt your pet and make him bleed. If your pet has dark nails, you may not be able to see the quick, which means you should trim only the smallest amount of nail to avoid cutting it.

4 Whatever color your guinea pig's nails are, trim only the tips of the nails with the trimmers. Try to take off just the hooked ends and leave the nails as smooth as possible. If you happen to cut too deeply, apply styptic powder to the cut nail to stop the bleeding.

Guinea Pig Grooming Supplies

These are the supplies you'll need to keep your guinea pig looking his best.

- soft bristle brush
  (for short-haired guinea pigs)
- metal comb or brush
  (for long-haired guinea pigs)
- guinea pig or small animal
  shampoo
- nail clippers
- styptic powder
- cotton swabs
- gentle ear cleanser
- scissors
- towel

Ensure his coat is completely dry before returning him to his cage. If your guinea pig is comfortable with it, blow-dry him (use the "warm" setting on the dryer to prevent burning him) to shorten drying time and to reduce the risk he may become chilled. While drying, be sure to keep the dryer about a foot away from his coat to reduce the chance he could

Long nails can impair your guinea pig's ability to walk correctly or can cause him injury, so trim them every 8-12 weeks.

overheat, and make sure to keep the power cord out of reach as it could be a chewing temptation to him. Keep the dryer moving to ensure your pet's hair gets dried as quickly as it can without exposing him to heat any longer than necessary.

Guinea pigs that are shown are more likely to be bathed than regular pet guinea pigs. Bathing is an important part of grooming for the show ring to ensure your pet looks his best. Preparing for a show also means that the coat is brushed thoroughly to make it shine and to remove dead hairs, and to make sure his eyes, ears, nose, and mouth (and the hair around them) are clean. His paws and nails also need to be washed and trimmed. Consult your local guinea pig club or the breeder you purchased your animal from for more information on how to get your pet ready for showing.

Nail Care

Guinea pigs have four toes on their front feet and three toes on their back feet. Each toe has a nail that requires regular monitoring and maintenance, and each nail grows continuously. If left untrimmed, toenails will become a hazard to your guinea pig because they can catch on something in his cage, which may cause him to bleed or even break a bone. In extreme cases, untrimmed nails curve around on themselves and press into your pet's paws, which may make it almost impossible for him to walk.

Check your guinea pig's nails weekly for signs of growth, and trim them every 8-12 weeks. If you're unsure how it's done, ask your veterinarian to demonstrate nail trimming before you try the procedure yourself.

Regular trimming means that the quick recedes in your pet's nail, which makes it less likely to be cut. It also gets you and your pet used to the process, which makes it easier to do over time.

Ear Care

Ear care should be part of your regular grooming routine because guinea pigs are prone to excessive wax buildup in their ears. For some animals, it's a perfectly normal condition, while for others excess wax could indicate problems such as an infection or a

Check your pet's teeth weekly to see that they line up correctly and are not overgrown.

mite infestation.

Examine your pet's ears carefully each day. Check to see the amount of wax present, and notice if they have any unusual odor or discharge coming from them. If they do, set up an appointment with your veterinarian.

Regular cleaning can help to keep the external parts of your guinea pig's ears healthy. To clean his ears, wet a cotton swab with a gentle ear cleanser (ask your veterinarian for a recommendation) and carefully wipe off the outer surfaces. Don't try to clean out the inside of your pet's ears—they are very delicate, and this is a task for your veterinarian, not you.

Dental Care

Because a guinea pig's teeth are open-rooted and grow continuously, it's important to keep an eye on them as they grow. Check your pet's teeth weekly to see that they line up correctly and are not overgrown. One of the most common medical problems in guinea pigs is malocclusion, or poor bite, which is caused by misaligned teeth.

Looking Good

Grooming for Good Health

A regular grooming routine can help you maintain your pet's health as well as his appearance. When you groom your guinea pig, take time to inspect his body and overall condition:

1 Monitor his weight: Does he feel too thin, too fat, or just right?

2 Examine your pet's coat and body: Are there any bald spots or any unusual lumps or bumps since you last groomed him?

3 Check his teeth: Are they in good condition or are they overgrown?

4 Check his eyes, ears, and nose: Does he have discharge from any or all of them?

Knowing what's normal for your pet and noticing changes in his appearance and routine are the first steps in maintaining his health. If you find something unusual, contact your vet. It's much easier to treat minor problems before they become serious health issues.

Grooming time offers an opportunity to build the bond of trust with your pet.

Looking Good

Guinea pigs have 20 teeth—10 upper and 10 lower—and these teeth must line up with one another in order for your pet to eat properly. Loss of appetite, weight loss, and slobbering can all indicate dental problems, so alert your veterinarian if you see any of these signs. He may have to trim or file your pet's teeth to correct the malocclusion. Although trimming is best left to professionals, owners can help keep their pets' teeth in condition by offering a variety of appropriate chew toys and a varied diet that includes carrots, hay, or alfalfa cubes.

Another dental problem to be aware of is molar spurs. These can occur if a guinea pig's teeth do not wear down evenly, especially if the animal has been fed a poor diet. Molar spurs are sharp points that are created on the molars, and they can damage the animal's tongue or cheeks. If you notice your pet is unable to keep food in his mouth or that he seems to have lost interest in eating, he may have a molar spur. A visit to your veterinarian is required to solve this problem.

If you begin grooming your pet while he is young, he will grow accustomed to regular handling.

Grooming Time Means Bonding Time

In addition to helping you maintain your guinea pig's coat and monitor his health, grooming is a wonderful opportunity to build the bond of trust between you and your pet. It's ideal one-on-one time—with your pet sitting on your lap being gently brushed, what could be better for him? Spending as much time with you as possible fulfills your pet's need for social interaction, which is an important aspect of his contentment and well-being.

Begin grooming your pet when he is young. Get him accustomed to having his teeth checked and his ears gently cleaned in addition to the brushing he'll probably come to expect. Handle his feet regularly (even when you don't trim his nails) so he'll be used to this part of the process. All of this training will make your regular grooming sessions easier, and your veterinarian will likely appreciate your efforts come exam time.

Since these little creatures are so cuddly, it won't be hard for you to find time to spoil your guinea pig with a little regular pampering. Both you and your pet will be the better for it!

Showing Your Guinea Pig

Guinea pig shows are hosted by clubs around the country. They offer owners a chance to enter their pets in competition to see which pig most closely matches the ARBA Standard of Perfection for cavies in the eyes of the judges.

Show guinea pigs must be in top condition physically. They must be extremely well-groomed and need calm temperaments in order to sit quietly during judging. Show guinea pigs must also be accustomed to being handled by strangers because judges will pick them up as they are being evaluated.

Short-haired guinea pigs are shown in show coops, which are small cages that sit on the judging table. Long-haired guinea pigs are shown on show boards, which are burlap-covered boards that allow judges to evaluate the condition and appearance of the animal's coat.

For more information on guinea pig shows, visit the American Rabbit Breeders website (www.arba.net) or the American Cavy Breeders website (www.acbaonline.com).

The Oil Gland

As part of your grooming routine, you'll need to check the area around your pet's oil gland, which is located on his rear, above where his tail would be (if he had one). Secretions from this gland allow guinea pigs to mark their territories with a scent only they can smell. The sticky wax-like substance can build up and cause irritation.

Some guinea pigs have very active oil glands, while many do not. If your pet has an active one, you'll need to keep his coat clean by using a degreasing dish detergent or a nonabrasive hand cleaner regularly. Be sure to rinse the cleaning product off your pet completely so he doesn't accidentally ingest any chemicals.

Show guinea pigs must be well-groomed and in top physical condition.

Chapter 5

Feeling Good

Guinea pigs are remarkably sturdy little animals, but they can become ill from time to time, and when they do, it's often a serious situation. Preventing your pet from becoming ill is often much easier than treating him after the fact, so it's important to locate a veterinarian who can evaluate and monitor your guinea pig's health as soon as you can after bringing him home.

To help your guinea pig maintain his health and live a long life, he'll need to visit a veterinarian at least once a year. If he's sick, he'll have to go more often in order to receive appropriate treatment to regain his health.

As a caring owner, you play an important role in your pet's health care team. It's up to you to learn what's normal for your pet's daily routine and his food and water consumption, and to take him to the veterinarian if you notice anything unusual or out of the ordinary in his behavior or appearance. You need to feed him the healthiest food you possibly can and provide him with plenty of fresh water every day. You also have to make sure his cage is clean and his surroundings are safe to ensure he doesn't fall ill or become injured.

How to Select a Veterinarian

Choosing a veterinarian to treat your guinea pig requires a little more work than selecting one to treat a cat or a dog. Guinea pigs have special health concerns and require a doctor with specialized knowledge of their dietary needs and medical issues.

Begin your search by asking the breeder or pet store staff where they take their animals for veterinary care. If you aren't able to do this, look in your telephone book under veterinarians and read the ads carefully. Some doctors say they treat guinea pigs in

their advertisements, but most do not. Look for those who treat pocket pets, exotics, or rodents because they are likely to have the specific knowledge your pet requires.

After you've located three to five possibilities, call the offices to inquire if the veterinarian treats guinea pigs specifically. Ask how many the office treats in a month and whether or not any of the vets own guinea pigs as personal pets. If you don't like the answers you receive, contact the next clinic on your list. If you feel that the answers you've received are good ones, make an appointment for your pet to be evaluated and see how the doctor handles him.

You may also be able to search online for veterinarians who treat guinea pigs in your area. Give your browser a few parameters, such as "guinea pig veterinarian [your city or state]," to help in your search.

Visiting the Doctor

Plan to arrive at the veterinary office about 30 minutes before your scheduled appointment because you will need to fill out some paperwork. After your paperwork is complete, you and your pet will be placed in an exam room to meet the veterinarian and some of the office staff.

A technician may come in ahead of the doctor to weigh your pet and take some basic information as to the reason for your visit. Answer these

First Aid for Your Guinea Pig

In certain emergency situations, your guinea pig will require first aid before he sees a vet. Although it's difficult to do, it's important that you remain calm while you are treating your pet so you can give him the best care possible.

Contact your vet's office for immediate instructions. Explain that you have an emergency and tell them clearly what has happened to your guinea pig. Listen carefully to what the staff tells you to do, and follow their instructions completely. Transport your pet quickly and safely to the animal clinic so he can be seen by experts as soon as possible.

If your pet is bleeding, control the bleeding with direct pressure, if possible, before transporting him to the doctor's office. If your pet appears to have a broken bone, wrap him in a towel and place him in a travel carrier or other small cage for transport.

If your pet has burned his skin by lying too close to a heater vent or other heat source, rinse the burned skin gently with cold water before taking him to the vet. If your pet has been burned by household chemicals, follow the instructions given by the veterinary clinic staff before transporting your pet for additional treatment.

Pet-proofing your home and being aware of your guinea pig's location whenever he is out of his cage will do a lot to ensure that he doesn't get into too many dangerous situations, but accidents do happen. By staying calm and following the instructions your veterinarian's office staff gives you, you can help your pet start off right on his road to recovery.

Not all veterinarians treat guinea pigs, so be sure to select an exotic animal specialist who will know how to care for your pet.

a more in-depth examination. During this hands-on check, he or she will examine your pet's eyes and ears, check his mouth and teeth, listen to his heart and lungs, and look over his feet and toes.

In addition to the hands-on examination, the veterinarian may order some routine tests. These may include blood workups or X rays. Ask him to explain how these tests can help in the diagnosis of your pet's

questions as honestly as you can because it will help the doctor get to know more about your guinea pig and his situation.

When the veterinarian comes in, he or she will visually examine your guinea pig in his travel cage for a few moments before taking him out for a closer look. This will give your pet a chance to become accustomed to him or her, as well as giving the vet an opportunity to see how your pet looks and acts before he is handled by a stranger.

After looking your animal over and talking to you about his condition, the doctor will take him out of his cage for

FAMILY-FRIENDLY TIP

A Visit to the Vet

To help your child understand what happens at the vet's office, you'll need to explain what will likely go on during the pet's examination. Explain that the doctor will weigh your pet, handle him carefully, and give him a physical that may include listening to his heart, checking his eyes and ears, and examining his teeth.

Technicians or nurses may be involved in the examination as well. The doctor and staff will probably ask questions about the guinea pig's diet and his normal daily activities, and you will have a chance to ask questions about his care (if you have any). The doctor may then recommend some tests, and he or she will set up a routine examination schedule for your pet.

condition, and also ask any other questions you may have about your pet's diet, grooming, or daily care. The staff can be valuable allies in your efforts to maintain your pet's health and well-being because they know the latest information on small animal care and nutrition.

After treatment options have been discussed and your questions have been answered, the veterinarian will tell you if any follow-up examinations are required. If your guinea pig is just having a routine exam, he or she will set up a schedule of well-pet checks to ensure his continued good health.

Regular checkups help to prevent potential health problems.

Signs of Illness

If your guinea pig becomes ill, he probably will not show any outward indications of illness immediately. Changes in his routine and appearance will likely happen more gradually because he is naturally conditioned to conceal any signs of sickness or weakness. Remember that in his native environment, your guinea pig is a prey animal, and any prey animal that shows weakness is quickly eaten by predators.

Be aware of your pet's normal routine, and don't hesitate to take him to the veterinarian if you notice something is different about his behavior or appearance. Illnesses that are caught early by observant owners are easier to treat than those that are

neglected for long periods of time, so it's important to act on any small indicators of trouble. Here are some things to be aware of that usually require immediate veterinary attention:

Change in stools: A change in the color or consistency of your pet's droppings is cause for concern. Also be aware of changes in the number of times your pet eliminates—suddenly going a lot more than he used to, or not eliminating as often as he used to are sure signs that something, possibly quite serious, is amiss.

Discharge from the eyes, ears, or nose: Your guinea pig's eyes, ears, and nose should be clean and free of discharge. If they are not, the cause (illness or injury) must be determined, and treatment may need to be provided.

Emergencies:

When Veterinary Intervention is a Must

Your guinea pig is a curious, active animal—that's part of what attracted you to him in the first place. Sometimes, though, his curiosity gets the better of him, and he may end up in a situation that requires emergency medical care.

1 Encounters with other animals can result in bite wounds that require medical attention. Their saliva may contain bacteria that are very toxic to your guinea pig, so your veterinarian may need to clean the wounds and prescribe medication that will help your pet heal.

2 Chewing on electrical cords can result in burns or electrocution, both of which may require immediate medical intervention. Protect your pet from harm by covering your electrical cords with conduit or other chew-proof covers.

3 Being stepped on or sat on can result in broken bones, internal bleeding, or internal injury. All of these require veterinary examination and treatment.

4 Temperature extremes can result in heatstroke (from being too hot) or frostbite (from being too cold). Both conditions require urgent medical care to help your pet recover.

5 Signs that your pet needs medical assistance include bleeding; gasping for breath; diarrhea; the inability to use one or more legs; staggering; the inability to walk; or severely irritated eyes, nose, or mouth. Discuss these conditions with your veterinarian before an emergency occurs so you'll know what to be on the lookout for and what to do to help your pet have the best chance at recovery.

Lethargy: If your normally active pet suddenly starts sitting like a lump in his cage, this can be an indication of poor health. Likewise, if your pet suddenly acts as if every move makes his body hurt, there may be a serious underlying cause requiring immediate attention.

Loss of hair: Hair loss is not a normal situation in guinea pigs and could be the result of a skin disorder, parasitic infestation, fungal infection, stress, pregnancy, or a poor diet.

Loss of interest in food or water: Most guinea pigs are "all about food," so it's significant if yours suddenly seems less interested in his food or stops eating altogether. If your pet suddenly stops drinking water, this can lead to dehydration, and he needs to be checked by your veterinarian right away.

Pain: If your guinea pig suddenly acts as though his entire body hurts, or if he reacts in pain when you touch him, he needs to be examined. If he sits in his cage in an unusual position, this can also indicate an illness or injury that needs to be evaluated.

Swelling: A swollen area on your guinea pig's body can be the result of an injury, parasite infestation, or an internal problem that could be quite serious like an abscess, cyst, or tumor.

Tooth or mouth problems: If your pet suddenly begins to drool excessively, or if his teeth seem to stick out of his mouth more than normal, he may need dental care to correct the problem.

A change in your guinea pig's behavior, appearance, or mood may indicate that he is ill.

69

Vocalizing: If your pet suddenly starts making more noise than normal, or he starts making noises that you've never heard him make before (especially if these noises sound like he's in pain), he's telling you something is wrong.

Any change in your guinea pig's normal appearance or routine can be an indicator of the onset of an illness. Take steps to help your pet as soon as you notice changes so he can have the best chance to recover quickly from whatever is ailing him.

Guinea Pig Illnesses

Guinea pigs can be prone to a few medical conditions and illnesses, including dental problems, digestive system disorders, eye injuries, foot problems, heatstroke, lumps, respiratory ailments, scurvy, and skin disorders. Let's look at each in a bit more detail.

Dental Problems

Because a guinea pig's teeth grow constantly, he is at risk for dental problems due to misalignment of the teeth. If left untreated, misaligned teeth can lead to an inability to eat, which means the guinea pig may starve to death.

Signs of dental problems can include a refusal to eat, drooling, or weight loss. Your veterinarian can usually treat a dental problem by regularly trimming your guinea pig's teeth to keep them at the proper length. This will allow your pet to eat normally and comfortably.

Digestive System Disorders

Digestive system problems can have a number of causes, including infections, stomach ulcers, poor diet, or antibiotic toxicity (most commonly prescribed

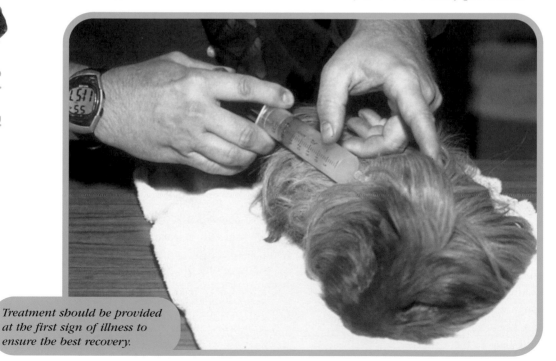

Treatment should be provided at the first sign of illness to ensure the best recovery.

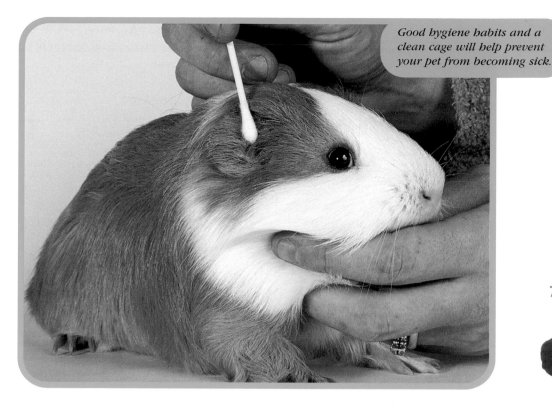

Good hygiene habits and a clean cage will help prevent your pet from becoming sick.

antibiotics are toxic to guinea pigs, so please discuss medications with your veterinarian before administering them to your pet).

The easiest way to determine whether or not your guinea pig has a problem with his digestive system is to check his droppings. If they do not appear normal in their size, shape, and consistency, you should make an appointment with your veterinarian immediately. If your guinea pig suddenly develops diarrhea or becomes constipated, these are also indications of a digestive disorder that may need immediate attention.

Eye Injuries/Disorders

Guinea pigs can be prone to eye injuries caused by tough hay stalks in their bedding or by wires that protrude from their cages. Their eyes may also become irritated by dusty bedding or by chemicals used to clean in and around their cages. To protect your pet's eyes from harm, make sure the bedding you give him is dust-free and does not contain items that could cause injury. Check his cage regularly for hazards, and make any necessary repairs as soon as possible.

If you notice your pet's eyes aren't as bright and clear as they normally are, contact your veterinarian for an immediate appointment. Many eye problems or infections can quickly become serious and may result in a loss of vision if left untreated.

Foot Problems

Your guinea pig spends all of his time on his feet, so foot problems can quickly become a dilemma for your pet. Environmental factors, such as a wire-mesh cage floor, can contribute to foot problems, as can poor husbandry or obesity.

To avoid this, make sure your pet maintains a healthy weight and has daily chances to exercise outside his cage. Provide him with an enclosure that has a solid bottom to help keep his feet free from injury.

If you notice your pet suddenly becomes lame or if his feet look red or swollen, take him to see the vet.

Heatstroke

Guinea pigs are not particularly heat-tolerant animals. As a result, they can be more prone to heatstroke than other household pets. They tend to overheat when the temperature rises above 75°F (23.9°C), especially if high humidity accompanies the higher temperatures.

Signs of heatstroke can include rapid breathing, drooling, and weakness. Affected guinea pigs tend to lie down flat and stretch themselves out. If you see signs of heatstroke in

your pet, contact your veterinarian's office immediately. You may be instructed to lower his body temperature before bringing him in. To do this, place him in a sink in a couple of inches of cool water. Hold him up so his head is out of the water and he can breathe, and then wrap him loosely in a towel for transport.

Heatstroke is easy to prevent. Check your pet's cage area regularly to ensure the room temperature is comfortable (between 65° and 75°F/18.3° and 23.9°C). Set up a fan nearby so you can easily turn it on if the room feels too warm. Don't put the cage near a sunny window or by a radiator or wood stove because your pet can easily overheat on a warm day or when the heat is on.

Lumps

Lumps are most often caused by a bacterial disease called *Streptococcus zooepidemicus.* This disease makes

Toxic Antibiotics

Guinea pigs have a delicate digestive system containing microorganisms that help them digest their food. Some antibiotics, especially various penicillins, are toxic to them. There are only a few safe antibiotics for guinea pigs, and these are usually quite effective. However, only your vet should administer medications to your pet.

your pet look as if he has the mumps, with swollen glands under his jaw. The swollen glands become abscessed, and the abscesses may break open.

Despite his swollen neck, your pet will usually act quite normal. However, the bacteria that cause the glands in his neck to swell are traveling throughout his body and may form abscesses in his internal organs that could be fatal. Lumps are also contagious to other guinea pigs, so isolate any sick animals from other pets in your home.

If your pet develops lumps, contact your veterinarian's office for an immediate appointment. They can often become a chronic problem, and surgery may be required to remove the affected glands and to treat the problem effectively. Antibiotic treatment may also be required to clear up the bacterial infection.

Respiratory System Problems

Your guinea pig has a delicate respiratory system that may leave him

Extra vitamin C may be necessary when your pet is recovering from an illness or during pregnancy.

prone to respiratory infections and pneumonia. Respiratory illness can spread quickly among guinea pigs, so separate any sick animals from the rest of your pets to ensure the health of all your companion animals.

Signs of respiratory illness include breathing difficulties, wheezing, a bloody or crusty discharge from the nose, and appetite loss. If you notice any of these symptoms in your pet, contact your veterinarian's office immediately. Respiratory illnesses can be fatal, and early treatment is essential if your pet is to recover.

Scurvy

Scurvy is a serious vitamin deficiency that can occur if your guinea pig does not receive adequate levels of vitamin C in his diet each day. This slow-developing disease affects the animal's bones and cartilage. Remember that guinea pigs cannot create enough vitamin C on their own to maintain good health and

Guinea Pig First Aid Kit

To help you prepare for an emergency, it's a good idea to create a first aid kit for your guinea pig. Here are some items to include:

- contact info for your vet
- clean towel
- gauze pads
- self-adhering bandage material
- first aid tape
- cotton balls
- cotton-tipped applicators
- scissors
- tweezers
- hot water bottle
- heating pad
- cold pack
- cornstarch
- petroleum jelly
- rectal thermometer
- hydrogen peroxide
- iodine
- rubbing alcohol
- triple antibiotic ointment
- small flashlight
- magnifying glass

Keep these items together in a tackle box or other easily accessible storage box. Keep your pet's travel carrier or another small cage next to the first aid kit so you have something to transport your guinea pig in if he becomes injured. Check the supplies regularly to ensure they have not expired, and replace any expired medications promptly.

Store the kit in a central location, such as a hall closet or under your pet's cage. Make sure all family members know where it is before an emergency occurs.

that their diets must be supplemented with it.

Signs of scurvy include joint pain, loose teeth, gum pain, appetite loss, and lumps on the rib cage. If left untreated, scurvy can be fatal to your pet, so it's important to contact your veterinarian's office promptly if you notice signs of this deficiency.

Fortunately, scurvy is easily prevented by offering your pet a diet that contains 15 to 25 milligrams of vitamin C each day (more if your pet is pregnant or recovering from illness or injury). Give him fresh guinea pig pellets, along with a selection of healthful fruits and vegetables on a regular basis, and you shouldn't have to worry.

Skin Disorders

Guinea pigs can suffer from skin problems caused by a number of factors, including a weakened immune system, an incomplete diet, allergies, or poor hygiene. These problems can also include external parasites, such as fleas or mites, and fungal infections.

If you notice that your pet's coat suddenly seems patchy and uneven, or if he suddenly becomes bald on parts of his body, contact your veterinarian's office for an appointment. Some fungi can be passed from guinea pigs to other members of the household, including people, so it's important to have your pet's skin problem diagnosed and treated quickly.

Guinea pigs can suffer from stress, so be sure to give your pet all the care and attention he deserves.

Trauma

Trauma is another common problem for guinea pigs. Even in the best homes, accidents happen, but by setting up a pet-proof area and monitoring your pet's activities when he is out of his cage, you can help greatly reduce the chances of your pet suffering a traumatic injury.

Stress

Stress can be a contributing factor to illness in your guinea pig. Some stressors are obvious, but others are less easily seen.

Poor nutrition creates stress on a guinea pig's body because he will lack vital nutrients needed to maintain good health. You can help reduce stress in this area by feeding a balanced, healthful diet and by keeping mealtimes on a regular schedule.

Dirty cages can be another stressor that leads to illness, so make sure your pet's enclosure is cleaned regularly. In addition to cleanliness, make sure your guinea pig's cage is not overcrowded with roommates, which can also create stress or worse scenarios.

Another stressor is the addition of new animals in your home, whether they are other guinea pigs or pets of another species. If your guinea pig smells new animal scents, he could fear that he is in danger from these new, unknown predators. Introduce him to the new pet cautiously, and monitor all interactions at first to ensure both parties get along. Never allow your guinea pig to be alone with other pets to protect the safety of all animals in your home.

Now let's consider where your pet's cage is located in your home. Is it placed in a cold or drafty spot, or is it in an area that's humid and overly warm? Either temperature extreme can create stress in your guinea pig's life, which can lead to illness if left unchanged. Make sure your pet is neither too cold nor too hot in his cage, and make sure it is in a part of your home that you spend time in regularly, such as a family room, to ensure your pet feels like he's part of your daily activities.

Travel is another potential stressor in your guinea pig's life. Try not to

Quarantine

If you own more than one guinea pig or have other pets, it is important to prevent disease or bacteria from spreading by keeping a sick animal isolated from other pets until he is given a clean bill of health by your vet. This is also necessary when adding a new animal to your collection, regardless of how good his former home was. Take your newly acquired pet to the vet for a thorough checkup before introducing him to his cagemates.

77

take him on too many unnecessary trips, and make arrangements for someone to care for him if you have to be away on a business trip or vacation. Guinea pigs like their home routines, so try to keep them as consistent as possible to help your pets stay healthy.

Other potential stressors can include loud noises, underlying health problems such as parasites, and the stresses of pregnancy and caring for young in a female guinea pig. Take steps to reduce stress as much as possible to help your pet stay healthy, and make sure he visits the veterinarian regularly.

Care of Older Guinea Pigs

Guinea pigs are considered to be "old pets" when they are four years or older. As they age, they require a little extra care to ensure their continued good health. Owners need to be a little more vigilant about daily care and nutrition when caring for a senior pet.

Owners of older female guinea pigs need to know that they will stop breeding when they are between three and four years of age. Unspayed females may develop ovarian cysts or breast tumors at this time, and these may need to be treated surgically.

Owners of older guinea pigs also need to be aware of a senior animal's

If you are housing guinea pigs together, make sure they are either neutered or they are of the same gender. If not, you will likely soon have a litter of babies on the way because guinea pigs are notorious for their breeding abilities.

If you have housed a male and a female guinea pig together and if the female is in season, chances are the guinea pigs will mate and the female will become pregnant. Litter sizes can range from one to eight babies (two to four offspring is the most common), which will be born after a 70- to 80-day gestation period.

If you suspect your guinea pig is pregnant, take her to the veterinarian's office for a checkup. Your vet can conduct tests to determine whether or not she is pregnant and offer suggestions on proper prenatal care.

One thing to keep in mind is that a pregnant guinea pig's vitamin C requirements will increase significantly. Your pregnant female will need at least 30 milligrams of vitamin C daily, so be sure to provide her with additional dietary sources of vitamin C to maintain her health and the health of her growing family.

Your guinea pig should be able to deliver her litter without difficulty, but be sure to discuss signs of trouble with your veterinarian so you'll know what to look for in case she requires assistance with her delivery.

If you are still housing your male and female guinea pigs together during pregnancy, you should remove the male about a week before the female is due to deliver. In some cases, the male's presence is a stressor on the female, which may complicate her delivery. In all cases, the female will come into season immediately after giving birth, and it's very difficult for a female guinea pig to carry back-to-back litters successfully.

tendency to develop skin problems, such as lice or mites. Although they may not have had such skin problems when they were younger, they may become prone to such infestations in later years. These infestations may be caused by a weakening of the immune system or because of changes in the animal's environment, such as more crowded living conditions or medical problems.

Another potential health issue for older guinea pigs is dental problems. In addition to overgrown teeth, an older guinea pig may suffer from arthritis of the jaw, which makes it more painful and difficult to chew. This, in turn, can aggravate an overgrown tooth because he is unwilling or unable to chew as much as he did when he was younger, which helped maintain his dental health in younger years. Such dental problems can also lead to the formation of abscesses in your pet's jaw, which will require veterinary treatment.

To help maintain good health in their later years, older guinea pigs should visit the veterinarian at least twice a year. These semi-annual visits can include a thorough examination of your pet's teeth and any routine maintenance needed, as well as providing an opportunity to monitor your pet's overall health through physical examinations and routine blood tests.

You can help make your senior guinea pig more comfortable by offering him a low-fat diet that consists mainly of timothy hay and green vegetables. This diet will help maintain his digestive health and keep his weight at a manageable level. Reduce the amount of pellets you feed, and ask your veterinarian to recommend the proper amount for your pet's particular age group.

Alter his normal routine only if it means making his life more comfortable. For example, if you used to handle him quite a bit, but his arthritis now seems to make him uncomfortable when you cuddle him, arrange to have him sit next to you on the couch on a special towel instead. This way, he can enjoy your companionship without being made uncomfortable.

Chapter 6

Being Good

Now that you know the basics of caring for your guinea pig, it's time to discuss how you'll tame and train him. Proper handling and careful training can strengthen the bond between you and your pet, and he'll find things more interesting if he can be taken out of his cage regularly. This can be one of the most enjoyable parts of owning a guinea pig, so be sure to make the process fun for both of you!

Handling Your Guinea Pig

The first step in training your pet is learning how to handle him safely. To pick up your guinea pig, you will need to use both hands, gently sandwiching his body between them. Your bottom hand and forearm support his spine and back legs, while your top hand keeps your pet secure as you remove him from his cage. Guinea pigs can be prone to back problems, so it's important to support his spine at all times. Hold him securely when returning him to his cage, too, because guinea pigs tend to become excited when they see their habitats and may try to jump out of your hands when headed home.

Whenever possible, hold your pet while you are seated. Walking with your guinea pig in your arms can be a risky proposition because he may try to jump away from you or wiggle free. His chances of injury are greatly reduced if you are seated while holding him. If you must carry him from his enclosure to other locations in your home, rest his body on your forearm for support. Point his head toward your hand, while keeping your other hand on his back to provide additional support. Hold your guinea pig close to your chest as you support him; this may help him feel more secure as you transport him.

Taming

Taming is the next step toward training your guinea pig. Most owners work on taming their pets and are content with being able to handle them comfortably. However, guinea pigs can be trained to do simple tricks, which we'll discuss shortly.

Taming your pet means that you handle him in a calm, gentle manner to get him used to being held and carried. You need to be patient with him as you begin this process because he may be a bit jumpy at first. His natural instincts

FAMILY-FRIENDLY TIP

Teaching a Child Proper Handling

Allowing a child to handle a pet depends greatly on his or her age. Young children (those under the age of 8) should not handle a guinea pig on their own. With supervision, they may hold him on their laps while seated on the floor, or they may pet him when he is out of his cage on an adult's lap.

Children age 8 and older should be able to handle a pet on their own. Take the time to teach them how to hold and carry a pet safely, and supervise interactions between them to ensure neither is injured. Don't allow older children to take your guinea pig out of his cage if you are not around, but let them hold and handle him when you are in the room.

tell him to try to run away from you, so you need to work with him gradually in order to teach him to trust you and enjoy being held. Remember, guinea pigs are normally prey animals in the wild, so their survival instincts may kick in at first and make them resistant.

When you first begin, you may want to hold your guinea pig on a towel in your lap as you sit on the floor, which may make it more comfortable for your pet and will also protect you from accidents if he becomes excited or frightened by the new situation. Being seated on the floor also helps to minimize any possible injuries should he try to jump out of your lap or run away.

Younger guinea pigs tame faster than adult animals, so it's best to begin as soon as you can. Adult animals may be a bit more difficult to deal with, especially if they have been mishandled, but with gentle, patient practice, you can even tame them.

One way to get a reluctant animal to accept handling is to offer him special food treats from your hand each day. Over time, he will realize that you are the provider of these goodies and will be more likely to come to you. Food is a good motivational aid, so try tempting your pet with a favorite healthy treat. Then, as he becomes more comfortable with you, alternate the treats with lavish praise so he doesn't come to expect a treat every time.

Children should be taught how pick up and properly carry a guinea pig before being permitted to handle one.

Spend a few minutes in the morning and in the evening each day working with your pet. Keeping the sessions short and positive will make the process more enjoyable for both of you, and your pet will learn what you want him to do more quickly. Your guinea pig has an attention span of 5 to 15 minutes, so try to keep your sessions about 10 minutes long each time you sit down to train him.

End each session on a positive note, even if it means just quietly holding your pet for a few minutes before you put him back in his cage. Give him a treat as well, because this will also help him learn to enjoy the taming process.

As you work with your pet, don't become angry with him, don't raise your voice, and never, ever hit him. You need to work on building trust in your guinea pig, and you will do this by being patient, quiet, and positive. These behaviors will send a positive message, and your pet will become

Tiny Tots and Training Basics

Your child can help you tame and train your guinea pig by behaving toward him the same way that you do: by approaching his cage quietly and speaking to him in a soothing, calm voice. He or she should pet the guinea pig gently and offer him treats, both when he's in his cage and when he's enjoying supervised out-of-cage time.

Your child can also help your pet meet new people by explaining to others how to act around him. Under supervision, you can have the child introduce the guinea pig to friends and allow them to give him treats if they behave properly.

If everyone acts in similar ways around your guinea pig, he will learn to expect consistent, gentle behavior from the people who care for him. In turn, he will be more comfortable around you because he trusts you to treat him in this way, and he will be a calmer, easier-to-handle pet as a result.

more comfortable with handling when he feels he can trust you to be kind to him.

If your guinea pig is still resistant, keep working with him to calm him down and get him used to being picked up, even briefly. He will need to be picked up and taken out of his cage

when you clean it and when he visits the veterinarian, and you will also need to become comfortable handling him during these and other times. Your guinea pig will also benefit from regular out-of-cage time during which he can explore his environment and run around for a little exercise, so being accustomed to handling is important to his overall well-being as part of your family.

Don't force your pet to be touched or cuddled excessively if he doesn't seem to enjoy it—just handle him as needed. Some guinea pigs don't enjoy being cuddled and petted, while others think it's the best thing an owner can do. You'll have to judge how your pet reacts to it and adjust to his preferences.

85

Proper handling and training can strengthen the bond between you and your pet.

Potty Training Procedure

It is possible to toilet train a guinea pig, but it's unlikely most owners will take the time to train their pets to this level. Toilet training a guinea pig can take one of two forms: You can train the animal to urinate in a certain spot in his cage, or you can train him not to urinate outside the cage. (Guinea pigs will defecate as needed, but their droppings are easily cleaned up.) The first behavior is much easier to achieve than the second, and patience is required on your part as you undertake the training process.

1 Most guinea pigs naturally urinate in one corner of their cage, which is why it may be easier to teach them to use a specific spot. After you determine where your pet urinates, set up a small litter box in that spot. When you see him using the litter box, praise him and reward him with treats after he's finished. If you find he uses another spot, pick up the used bedding with a small scoop and place it in the litter box. In time, your pet should catch on that he's supposed to use the litter box as his toilet.

2 Training a guinea pig not to urinate outside his cage is a bit more problematic, simply because guinea pigs have very small bladders. They must urinate about every 15 minutes, which can make it difficult to teach them to only go in their litter boxes. In this case, owners have to learn which behaviors indicate a need for them to urinate and train themselves to put the animals back in their cages at the appropriate times. Signs of impending urination include fidgeting, backing up, or gentle nips. All these actions indicate that your pet has to relieve himself, and if you don't put him back in his cage, he will go wherever he is. Praise your pet when he urinates in the cage, but don't scold him if he has an accident. Accidents are not your guinea pig's fault—you need to learn to be more observant of his behavior and take quick action when you see he needs to go to the bathroom to make this type of toilet training successful.

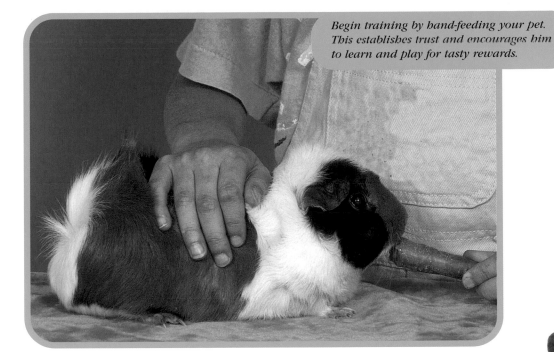

Begin training by hand-feeding your pet. This establishes trust and encourages him to learn and play for tasty rewards.

Training

Positive Reinforcement

You will get the best results from the taming or training process if you give your pet positive reinforcement, such as special treats, lavish praise, and extra cuddling or petting (if he enjoys being handled).

Like most animals, guinea pigs respond only to positive reinforcement—you cannot will your pet to do what you want him to, and you can't punish him into good behavior. He only understands being rewarded when he does something right, so you need to encourage him into good behavior by praising him or giving him a treat when he performs as you want him to. Punishing your guinea pig only teaches him that people are mean and bad and that he should try to get away from them at all costs.

Tricks to Teach Your Guinea Pig

Guinea pigs can learn a variety of tricks, but not all of them are tricksters. If your pet is a calm animal that enjoys being around people and being handled and petted, he will probably be a good candidate for trick training. If he is shy and skittish, don't force him to learn tricks because he may become stressed by the training process.

Treats as a Training Tool

Treats are a great motivational tool and one of the best things you can use to help in taming or training your pet. Most guinea pigs have healthy appetites, so they can be easily tempted into good behavior with the promise of a tasty reward. In training, treats can be used as a lure to coax your pet into doing something you want him to do and must be given as positive reinforcement when your pet performs as you ask. By rewarding your pet's good behavior with food initially, you make him more likely to repeat the behavior. Once your pet is behaving well, alternate food with verbal praise or cuddling to ensure he will continue to do what you want without causing him to become overweight from consuming too many goodies.

One of the easiest tricks to teach your guinea pig is to have him respond to being called. Hold a treat in your hand and call him by his name. Encourage him to come to you by saying "come here" and by speaking in a bright, positive voice. Reward him with the treat when he comes to you. Practice this routine daily, and alternate the food treat with verbal praise and cuddling as he becomes more comfortable coming to you.

Another trick your guinea pig can learn is to sit up and beg. Here again, use a food treat to tempt your pet into a sitting position. Practice with him until he sits still well, rewarding him with a treat or verbal praise. As you progress with your training, hold the treat just out of reach until he sits up and begs. This will take some time to teach because you will have to work up to having your pet sit up slowly. Guinea pigs cannot balance well on their back legs, and their bottoms are not designed for sitting up, but you can get them to pose briefly in a begging position if you work up to it patiently.

Another trick to teach your guinea pig is how to hop through a hoop. You will need a smooth-sided hoop that's large enough to let your guinea pig pass through it without hitting the sides with his body. You can use an embroidery hoop or you can fashion one out of stiff rope or wire; make sure there are no sharp edges that can cut your pet.

To begin training, place the hoop on its edge on the floor in front of your pet, and hold a treat out for him on the other side of it. Praise him and reward him with it when he walks through the hoop. If he's a little reluctant to go

Lose Your Guinea Pig

Because guinea pigs are larger than other pocket pets, such as hamsters or gerbils, they are less likely to become lost in your home. However, they can cause a commotion if they end up under a large, unmovable piece of furniture, such as a king-size bed or an entertainment center, so it's important to have any potential routes to hiding places blocked off before you give your pet out-of-cage time. Put a pillow across the bottom of your entertainment center, for example, or put 2 x 4s under your bed to prevent your pet from running into hard-to-reach places.

Buying or making a playpen for your pet can help contain him safely during his out-of-cage time. You can purchase one at your pet supply store, or you can use a child's inflatable wading pool filled with bedding to give your pet a place to play without having to worry he will run under or behind a large piece of furniture.

If your pet escapes and ends up in a place you can't easily reach him, shake a treat bag or put out some of his favorite goodies just beyond the object he's hiding under or behind. Step away from the area in which he's hiding, and call his name sweetly to encourage him to come out. In time, his curiosity and love of treats will likely coax him out of hiding and back into your arms.

Remember, inside or out, your guinea pig should always be supervised during out-of-cage time.

through the first time, you may need to have an assistant help with this step by gently nudging him through the first few times. Repeat the process until he is comfortable doing it, then slowly raise the hoop up a bit. Guinea pigs are comfortable hopping about an inch off the ground, so don't raise it any more than that at any time during training. Praise and reward your pet with treats when he performs well.

Walking Your Guinea Pig on a Leash

Believe it or not, you can train a guinea pig to walk on a leash. The key to success is finding the right leash to fit your pet properly. Rather than a conventional leash and collar arrangement that would be used on a dog's neck, you need to look at a mesh harness that fits around the guinea pig's torso so he isn't choked by it as he walks. Ask your veterinarian or the staff of the pet supply store for recommendations on the type of harness that's best for your particular pet.

Once you've selected the harness and put it on him, you'll find that he's quite fast on the ground. Despite their round bodies, guinea pigs are actually speedy, can take corners well, and change direction quickly, so it's a good idea to have a leash and harness on your pet to help control him when you take him out of his familiar surroundings (like when he goes to the veterinarian's office for a checkup).

A pen can contain your pets safely during out-of-cage playtime. Never leave them unsupervised outdoors.

If you plan to walk your guinea pig on a leash outside, be sure the outdoor temperature is between 60° and 80°F (15.6°-26.7°C) and that it isn't overly humid. Take your walks early in the morning or evening to avoid extreme midday heat. Keep your guinea pig away from grassy areas that could be contaminated by lawn chemicals or waste from other pets, and make sure he doesn't chew on any plants that may be poisonous. Also be sure to protect him from other curious animals—leashed or unleashed—that you may encounter by keeping a watchful eye. Keep your walks brief, about 10 minutes maximum, or stop sooner if you see your guinea pig becoming overheated.

Keep in mind that not all guinea pigs will become leash-trained. Try a leash and harness on your pet to see if he's comfortable wearing it (You should be able to slip a finger between the harness and his body.) Then, work with him each day to help him become more adjusted to it. If he still seems resistant after a couple of

Usually, a problem behavior indicates something is troubling your guinea pig or causing him discomfort.

weeks of training, it may be better if you stop trying to leash-train him and just accept him for the wonderful creature he is.

Some owners find that their guinea pigs enjoy walking on a leash indoors. This can be a wonderful way to give him exercise, especially when the weather does not permit outdoor time, along with the supervision he needs to keep him safe in the confines of your home.

Problem Behaviors

A guinea pig behavior, such as biting, may seem like a problem to us, but it may be a perfectly normal behavior for your pet. Guinea pigs only have a few ways to tell us if something is wrong with their surroundings—they can run away from us, they can vocalize loudly, or they can bite us.

If your pet begins biting you, take time to view the world from his perspective. What is different or frightening about his environment that's causing him to bite you? Has something changed with his health that makes it painful for you to hold or pet him? Stop and think how your pet views you and his surroundings, and take steps to change whatever is causing him to feel stressed enough to bite you. If you suspect something is physically wrong, contact your veterinarian's office for an appointment. Biting problems often resolve themselves when the underlying problem is solved. For instance, a guinea pig with external parasites may find it very painful to be petted until the parasites are cleared up.

Another behavior that we may consider a problem is chewing. This is also a completely normal behavior for your guinea pig. He needs to chew things constantly to keep his teeth in

shape, so make sure he has plenty of hay in his cage and safe chew toys to play with. This will help protect the items in your home that you don't want to be chewed, while ensuring he stays healthy and his teeth are in tip-top condition!

Keeping Peace in the Household

Bringing a guinea pig into your home means a period of adjustment while he gets used to you and you get used to having him around, too. If you have other pets in the home, they will also have to adjust to having the guinea pig in the house. The following are some tips to help you keep the peace in your animal kingdom.

Dogs: The amount of interest a dog displays in a guinea pig seems to vary by breed. Terriers, most hounds, and sporting breeds may see a guinea pig as potential quarry and may be tempted to hunt him instinctively, while herding or working breeds may want to herd or protect him from harm. Toy breeds may view the guinea pig as an equal because of their similar sizes and may bond well with him. Supervise all interactions between your dog and your guinea pig to protect the health of both animals.

Cats: Some cats seem very interested in guinea pigs and may view them as potential prey, while others act as if they'd rather snuggle with them for a nap than harm them. Use caution when introducing a cat and a guinea pig, and supervise all interactions between them.

Popcorning

One common guinea pig behavior that may be unfamiliar to a new owner is popcorning. Sometimes, a guinea pig will begin hopping all over his cage, skipping and running around. While he may seem alarmed or upset, he's actually happy and content in his surroundings. Fanciers describe this behavior as popcorning because the happy guinea pig resembles a kernel of corn being popped.

Supervise all interactions between household pets until they have adjusted to each other.

Birds: Birds and guinea pigs normally get along well together, but please supervise all interactions to ensure that a playful parrot doesn't accidentally injure your guinea pig with a lighthearted nip from its beak.

Rabbits: Although you might think rabbits and guinea pigs would live together well, they actually do not. Rabbits tend to be territorial, and they may injure a guinea pig that enters their space by kicking or biting him. Rabbits can also carry a bacterium called bordetella, which can cause pneumonia in guinea pigs.

Hamsters: Hamsters and guinea pigs should never be housed together in the same cage. They have completely opposite sleep and activity schedules, and hamsters tend to be nippy when they are awakened from a nap. They also have different dietary requirements, which would make sharing a cage problematic. They can, however, be kept in the same house as long as they are not allowed to socialize together.

Ferrets: Ferrets were originally bred to hunt small rodents, so it is unwise to keep a guinea pig and a ferret in the same home. Your guinea pig will likely become stressed from being around the ferret, and the ferret may be tempted to try to attack the guinea pig because it views your pet as a meal.

The Travel Carrier

A Home Away From Home

A travel carrier can be a very useful accessory for your guinea pig. You can use it to take him to the veterinarian, and you can also use it as a temporary holding cage.

Some guinea pigs take to their travel carriers right away, while others require more convincing that it is a safe place to stay. To help your pet become accustomed to it, leave it near his primary cage for a few days, then let him explore it during out-of-cage time. Leave the door on the carrier open at first so your guinea pig can go in and out of it freely. Put a few favorite treats in it to entice your pet to go in and explore it.

When he goes in and out of the carrier willingly, try closing the door behind him so he can become accustomed to his new surroundings. In most cases, he probably won't even notice he's closed in, but if he does, praise him for being a brave guinea pig and reassure him that he's fine. Open the door and let him out while continuing to tell him he's a good pet.

Continue to reinforce the idea that the carrier is a good place for your pet by leaving him in it for slightly longer periods with the door closed. In no time at all, he should be content and comfortable in his home away from home.

Your guinea pig will need a few days to adjust to his new home.

95

Being Good

Herps: Larger lizards and snakes may view a guinea pig as food and may cause your guinea pig to become stressed, while frogs and smaller lizards likely will cause no harm to him.

Supervise all interactions between your guinea pig and your reptile or amphibian pets to protect the health and well-being of all animals.

Patience, Repetition, and Motivation

Many people think that because guinea pigs are small rodents they are incapable of learning or being trained—and that is just not true! Any pet can learn if the owner keeps these training basics in mind: patience, repetition, and motivation. It's also important to remember that training sessions should be fun for both you and your pet. Don't expect too much too soon, and never scold your guinea pig if he doesn't perform as you'd like. Your first goal is to establish trust. You can motivate your pet to perform by giving him a healthy treat when he does well and, eventually, substitute treats with lavish praise or cuddles. For best results, keep sessions short, positive, and practice every day.

Glossary

Abyssinian—A guinea pig with hair that grows in swirls to form rosettes all over the body.

Agouti—The color of the original, wild guinea pigs. Each hair has two separate color bands and the tips of the hairs are dark, creating a "ticked" appearance.

alfalfa—A plant used as a food source for guinea pigs as hay or in pelleted feed.

Alpaca—A Peruvian guinea pig that carries the Rex gene, which causes the coat to be curly.

American—The name used for smooth-coated guinea pigs in the United States.

ascorbic acid—Vitamin C.

bale—A large bag of wood shavings used as cage bedding.

belly band—The non-ticked area of an Agouti.

boar—A male guinea pig.

bonnet strings—Streaks of non-ticked hair coming down from the chin on an Agouti—considered a fault.

Boucle—The North American name for the Alpaca.

bumblefoot—The swelling of a guinea pig's foot when bacteria enter small lesions on the foot pad.

cataract—A cloudy white film covering the lens of the eye.

carrier—A small, specially made cage used for transporting animals.

Cavia porcellus—The scientific name for the guinea pig.

cavy—A tailless rodent from South America, also the proper name for the guinea pig.

checkerboard pattern—The ideal pattern of markings on a tortoiseshell guinea pig.

chirping—A high-pitched sound usually made only by female guinea pigs, most often during the night.

cloudy tears—Milky discharge that appears in the corner of the eye when the eye is irritated and is flushing itself out.

collagen—A protein found in the bones that is necessary for growth and proper development.

coprophagy—The term used to describe when a guinea pig eats his own droppings to reabsorb valuable vitamins.

Coronet—A crested Silky.

crest—A single rosette of hair on the top of a guinea pig's head.

dilute—The lighter shade of a dark color such as black or brown.

diurnal—Awake during the day.

Duncan-Hartley—A special line of white guinea pigs used in medical research.

ear tag—A permanent metal clip or temporary adhesive label used to identify purebred show cavies.

English—The name used for smooth-coated guinea pigs in Europe.

estrus—The period of time when a female guinea pig is capable of conceiving.

exotic animal specialist—A veterinarian with the special training to care for guinea pigs and other small pets.

free feed—The term used for any food that is always made available to a guinea pig so that he may eat as much as he wants to.

frizzle—A long-haired cavy crossed with a Teddy.

frontal—The long fringe of hair covering a Peruvian's face.

gestation—The length of time from conception to birth.

grease spot—A spot of sticky hair on a guinea pig's rump caused by secretions from the oil gland.

impaction—A condition that affects males when they are unable to pass softer droppings and they become trapped in the skin fold of the anus, causing a painful lump.

incisors—A guinea pig's front teeth.

in-pig—The term used to describe a pregnant guinea pig.

intermediate—Young cavies up to 6 months of age.

junior—Young cavies up to 4 months of age.

leg—A special award won at a sanctioned cavy show. After three legs are earned, the owner may apply for a Grand Champion Certificate.

malocclusion—Improper alignment of the teeth.

marked—Cavies with specific patterns and markings arranged in an orderly fashion.

Merino—A crested Texel.

mites—Tiny parasites that burrow in the skin and inside the ears, causing itching and irritation.

molars—The guinea pig's back teeth, used for grinding food.

nest box—A small, floorless box usually made from wood, with windows and a door, placed inside the guinea pig's cage for hiding and sleeping.

neuter—A surgical procedure that alters a male so that he cannot reproduce.

otoscope—An instrument used by a veterinarian to look inside the mouth and ears.

pecking order—A system of rank found in multiple-guinea pig dwellings.

pedigree—The recorded line of the family descendents of a purebred cavy.

pellets—Prepared guinea pig food that is the foundation of a guinea pig's diet.

Peruvian—A cavy with long hair that grows forward over the body from rosettes (preferably only two) on the rump.

piglets—Baby guinea pigs.

points—The extremities of a cavy's body (ears, nose, and feet) that are sometimes darker than the rest of the body.

purring—An affectionate sound made by a guinea pig.

quick—The living tissue inside the toenails.

rare variety—A new breed of cavy that is not officially recognized.

Rex—A cavy with kinked, plush hair, bred in Europe.

rosette—The swirl of hair found on the Abyssinian.

run—An outdoor enclosure with an open floor that allows guinea pigs to graze.

salmonella—A harmful food bacteria.

sanctioned—A type of cavy show held under the authorization of a specific club or organization.

Satin—A variety of cavy with a glossy coat due to hollow hair shafts that reflect the light.

scurvy—The harmful condition that is the result of vitamin C deficiency.

Self—A variety of cavy that is the same color all over the entire body.

senior—A cavy that is more than 4 years old.

Sheltie—A cavy with long hair that grows straight, without swirls.

Silky—The North American name for the Sheltie.

sipper tube—The drinking device on a water bottle.

slicker—A brush with soft, wire bristles set close together, for grooming thick-coated cavies.

smooth coat—A cavy with short, smooth hair.

sodium ascorbate—Vitamin C crystals.

sow—A female guinea pig.

standard of perfection—A guideline that purebred cavies are judged against.

standards committee—A group of people within a cavy club who decide whether or not a new breed is to be accepted or standardized.

styptic powder—A special powder that clots the blood on the toenails if the quick has been cut.

sweep—The long hair that flows past the sides and rump of a cavy.

Teddy—A cavy with kinked, plush hair, bred in North America. Similar in appearance to the Rex, but genetically, different.

Texel—A long-haired Rex cavy.

ticked—The appearance of the dark hair tips of the Agouti.

timothy grass—A particular type of grass that hay for guinea pigs is made from.

Resources

Clubs and Societies

American Cavy Breeders Association
16540 Hogan Avenue
Hastings, MN 55033
Telephone: (612) 437-5041
www.acbaonline.com

**American Rabbit Breeders
Association, Inc.**
P.O. Box 426
Bloomington, IL 61702
Telephone : (309) 664-7500
Fax: (309) 664-0941
ARBAPost@aol.com
www.arba.net

**Golden State Cavy Breeders
Association, Inc.**
1360 Sawtooth Drive
Hollister, CA 95023
www.cavyweb.com/golden.htm

Mid-Atlantic Cavy Breeders Association
826 Anderson Street
Trenton, NJ 08611
www.macbapa.tripod.com

National Cavy Club/Cavies Magazine
Onley Park Cottage
Yardley Road
Olney, Bucks HP 13 5 NN
England
cavies@compuserve.com

New Zealand Cavy Club, Inc.
423 High Street South
Carterton, NZ

**North Carolina Cavy Breeders
Association**
228 Packs Road
Glenville, NC 28736
Telephone : (828) 743-2809
www.jnsg.servehttp.com/nccavy/

North Queensland Cavy Club, Inc.
PO Box 683
Aitkenvale, Queensland 4814
Australia

Ontario Cavy Club
63 River Street
Parry Sound, ONT P2A 2TS
Canada
www. cavy club.tripod.com

Rescue and Adoption Organizations

**American Society for the Prevention
of Cruelty to Animals**
424 East 92nd Street
New York, NY 10128-6801
(212) 876-7700
www.aspca.org
information@aspca.org

American Humane Association (AHA)
63 Inverness Drive East
Englewood, CO 80112
Telephone: (303) 792-9900
Fax: 792-5333
www.americanhumane.org

**Humane Society of the
United States (HSUS)**
2100 L Street, NW
Washington, DC 20037
Telephone : (202)- 452-1100
www.hsus.org

**Royal Society for the Prevention
of Cruelty to Animals (RSPCA)**
Telephone: 0870 3335 999
Fax: 0870 7530 284
www.rspca.org.uk

Emergency Services

**ASPCA Animal Poison
Control Center**
1717 South Philo Rd., Ste. 36
Urbana, IL 61802
1-888-426-4435
www.aspca.org

**North Shore Animal League America
and PROSAR International Animal
Poison Hotline**
vetmedicine.about.com
(888) 232-8870

Veterinary and
Health Resources

**Academy of Veterinary
Homeopathy (AVH)**
P.O. Box 9280
Wilmington, DE 19809
Telephone: (866) 652-1590
Fax: (866) 652-1590
E-mail: office@TheAVH.org
www.theavh.org

**American Academy of Veterinary
Acupuncture (AAVA)**
100 Roscommon Drive, Suite 320
Middletown, CT 06457
Telephone: (860) 635-6300
Fax: (860) 635-6400
E-mail: office@aava.org
www.aava.org

**American Animal Hospital
Association (AAHA)**
P.O. Box 150899
Denver, CO 80215-0899
Telephone: (303) 986-2800
Fax: (303) 986-1700
E-mail: info@aahanet.org
www.aahanet.org/index.cfm

**American College of Veterinary Internal
Medicine (ACVIM)**
1997 Wadsworth Blvd., Suite A
Lakewood, CO 80214-5293
Telephone: (800) 245-9081
Fax: (303) 231-0880
Email: ACVIM@ACVIM.org
www.acvim.org

American College of Veterinary
Ophthalmologists (ACVO)
P.O. Box 1311
Meridian, Idaho 83860
Telephone: (208) 466-7624
Fax: (208) 466-7693
E-mail: office@acvo.com
www.acvo.com

American Holistic Veterinary Medical
Association (AHVMA)
2218 Old Emmorton Road
Bel Air, MD 21015
Telephone: (410) 569-0795
Fax: (410) 569-2346
E-mail: office@ahvma.org
www.ahvma.org

American Veterinary Chiropractic
Association (AVCA)
442154 E 140 Rd.
Bluejacket, OK 74333
Telephone: (918) 784-2231
E-mail: amvetchiro@aol.com
www.animalchiropractic.org

American Veterinary Medical
Association (AVMA)
1931 North Meacham Road – Suite 100
Schaumburg, IL 60173
Telephone: (847) 925-8070
Fax: (847) 925-1329
E-mail: avmainfo@avma.org
www.avma.org

Animal Behavior Society
Indiana University
2611 East 10th Street #170
Bloomington IN   47408-2603
Telephone: (812) 856-5541
E-mail: aboffice@indiana.edu
www.animalbehavior.org

ASPCA Animal Poison Control Center
1717 South Philo Road, Suite 36
Urbana, IL 61802
Telephone: (888) 426-4435
www.aspca.org

British Veterinary Association (BVA)
7 Mansfield Street
London
W1G 9NQ
Telephone: 020 7636 6541
Fax: 020 7436 2970
E-mail: bvahq@bva.co.uk
www.bva.co.uk

Orthopedic Foundation
for Animals (OFA)
2300 NE Nifong Blvd
Columbus, Missouri 65201-3856
Telephone: (573) 442-0418
Fax: (573) 875-5073
Email: ofa@offa.org
www.offa.org

Publications

Magazines

Cavies Magazine
National Cavy Club
Olney
England
cavies@compuserve.com

Books

Barrie, Annmarie, *Guinea Pigs...Getting Started,* TFH Publications, Inc.

Bawoll, Karen, *A New Owners Guide to Guinea Pigs,* TFH Publications, Inc.

Burden, Margaret, *Guinea Pig Iopaedia,* Interpet Publishing.

Edsel, Jr., Graham, *The Guide to Owning a Guinea Pig,* TFH Publications, Inc.

Henwood, Chris, *Pet Owner's Guide to the Guinea Pig,* Interpet Publishing.

Page, Gill, *Getting to Know Your Guinea Pig,* Interpet Publishing.

TFH Staff Experts, *Quick & Easy Guinea Pig Care,* TFH Publications, Inc.

Internet Resources

www.cavies.org
This website has links to clubs, care sheets, tips, pet hotels, and supplies.

www.national cavy club.co.uk
Website for the National Cavy Club, UK. The aims of the club are basically to promote and encourage the keeping, breeding and exhibiting of all varieties of cavies to their standards of perfection and to protect and further the interest of all cavy fanciers. To further these aims, the NCC holds its Championship Show, incorporating three Stock Shows each year and five Area Shows.

www.caviesgalore.com
Cavies Galore: A Global Guinea Pig Community
An interactive guinea pig site with polls, message boards, and games. There's also a comprehensive cavy FAQ.

www.cavyinfo.com
This website primarily contains health information and healthcare for guinea pigs, including emergency care and finding a good exotic/small pet veterinarian

www.cavyland.org.uk
This website has links to clubs, care sheets, tips, pet hotels, and supplies.

www.cavymadness.com
Information for first time and current guinea pig owners including care and maintenance recommendations

www.cavyrescue.com
Linked to Pigloo.net, this is a rescue-friendly guinea pig on-line community. Since this site was started by rescuers and people who support the guinea pig rescue cause, this forum is rescue-friendly, which by definition means it is anti-breeding in sentiment. Note there is NO guinea pig breeding forum. However, if you wish to acquire a guinea pig, there are several places on the net to look for a humane source of guinea pigs. A few are:
Cavy Rescue: http://cavyrescue.com/
Guinea Pig Adoption Network: http://gpan.net

www.healthypet.com
Healthypet.com is part of the American Animal Hospital Association, an organization of more than 29,000 veterinary care providers committed to providing excellence in small animal care.

www.petfinder.org
Petfinder.org provides an extensive database of adoptable animals, shelters, and rescue groups around the country. You can also post classified ads for lost or found pets, pets wanted, and pets needing homes.

www.1888pets911.org
Pets 911offers a comprehensive database of lost and found pets, adoption information, pet health, and shelter and rescue information. The website also runs a toll-free phone hotline (1-888-PETS-911) that gives pet owners access to important life-saving information.

www.pet-net.net/small_animals/rabbits.htm
The Small Animal Pages website provides rabbit owners with a variety of pet information, chat groups, humor pages, and links to rescue groups and numerous other rabbit-related websites.

www.vin.com/vetquest/index0.html
VetQuest is an online veterinary search and referral service. You can search its database for over 25,000 veterinary hospitals and clinics all over the world. The service places special emphasis on veterinarians with advanced online access to the latest health care information and highly qualified veterinary specialists and consultants.

Save-A-Piggie
www.guineapigs.org/
This website is dedicated to helping guinea pig causes and rescue organizations.

Index

Index

Index

About the Author

Julie Mancini has authored numerous books and magazine and online articles, with animals as her primary focus. Pets have been an important part of her life since she was a child. Her first pet was a parakeet named Charlie, and since then, Julie has had many companion animals, including a guinea pig named Sweet Pea. Julie has been a freelance writer for the past 10 years. She and her husband currently live on a small acreage in south-central Iowa, where they plan to raise alpacas.

Photo Credits